Transcribing the Sound of English

Do you have a fear of transcription? Are you daunted by the prospect of learning and handling unfamiliar symbols? This workbook is for students who are new to linguistics and phonetics, and offers a didactic approach to the study and transcription of the words, rhythm and intonation of English. It can be used independently or in class and covers all the pronunciation details of words, phrases, rhythm and intonation. Progress is deliberately gentle with plenty of explanations, examples and 'can't go wrong' exercises. In addition, there is an associated website with audio recordings of authentic speech, which provide back-up throughout. The audio clips also introduce students to variations in accents, with eleven different speakers. Going beyond the transcription of words, the book also ventures into real discourse with the simplification systems of colloquial English speech, rhythm and intonation.

PAUL TENCH was senior lecturer in phonetics and applied linguistics at the Centre for Language and Communication Research, Cardiff University, and is now retired as an associate researcher there.

Transcribing the Sound of English

A Phonetics Workbook for Words and Discourse

PAUL TENCH

Cardiff University

CAMBRIDGE
UNIVERSITY PRESS

CAMBRIDGE UNIVERSITY PRESS
Cambridge, New York, Melbourne, Madrid, Cape Town,
Singapore, São Paulo, Delhi, Tokyo, Mexico City

Cambridge University Press
The Edinburgh Building, Cambridge CB2 8RU, UK

Published in the United States of America by Cambridge University Press, New York

www.cambridge.org
Information on this title: www.cambridge.org/9780521166058

First published 2011

Printed in the United Kingdom at the University Press, Cambridge

A catalogue record for this publication is available from the British Library

ISBN 978-0-521-16605-8 Paperback
ISBN 978-1-107-00019-3 Hardback

Additional resources for this publication at www.cambridge.org/tench

CONTENTS

v

ACKNOWLEDGEMENTS

Thanks

to colleagues in the *Centre for Language and Communication Research* at Cardiff University who encouraged me, especially to Dr Gerard O'Grady who checked through a lot of the work and helped with recordings,

to Dean, Nathan and Rob, our good natured and *very* patient technical staff,

to Jill Knight who helped with a lot of the typing,

to the two Tims, Maureen, Lisa, Chris, Shona, Gordon, Jennifer, Judy, Bhaskarrao and Wayne for agreeing to recording their voices in lexical sets and Su Yanling for recording Chinese lexical tones,

to Cambridge University Press and the authors, Ronald Carter and Michael McCarthy, of *Exploring Spoken English* for permission to use a number of their recordings, and

to the hundreds of undergraduate students of *Pronunciation of English* and the scores of postgraduates of *Phonology* who persevered with the material and gave me excellent feedback.

Introduction

Transcribing the Sound of English is not so much a coursebook in phonetics nor a textbook on English phonology, but a training course in developing students' powers of observation on features of English pronunciation and their skills in recording them in writing. It begins in a very elementary way but it is thorough, and eventually leads to the most comprehensive coverage of the sounds of English from words to full discourse that is available anywhere. It is designed for both native and non-native speakers of English, and for that latter reason all of the material is available in audio form. Every single word and all the discourses that are presented in *Transcribing the Sound of English* have been recorded and are available at www.cambridge.org/tench. Every single example with a reference number in the left-hand margin of this book is found with that same reference on that website.

If you are new to the subject, start at the beginning of Part I and do Chapters 1, 2 and 3 about transcribing words. You are introduced to broad transcription in a very gentle way, with plenty of practice material – so much, in fact, that a skilful, confident student could actually skip some of it, but there is enough to provide a less confident student with plenty of practice to build up their confidence. There is no key to this practice material, because you cannot go wrong! There are, however, quick tests (**kwɪk tɛsts**) at strategic points, and for them a key is provided on the same website. By the end of Chapter 3, you should be able to transcribe a word like *homogeneous* without any difficulty.

You could then choose to ignore Chapter 4 if you do not need to get into narrow transcription. You could also ignore Chapter 5 on accents if desired. These two chapters are more advanced and are written in a more academic style. But you could return to them later.

It would be good to do Chapter 6 on phrases, which returns to a more gentle approach in broad transcription. It introduces you to features of pronunciation that may not be immediately obvious when words come together and affect each other. But it only takes a little reflection to see what quite naturally happens in your own ordinary, informal speech.

Part II takes you on from words and phrases to full discourse with its rhythm and intonation systems. Chapter 7 shows the effect of rhythm in utterances, especially in terms of the so-called weak forms of words in context. It is closed with three whole discourses, monologues, which are carefully graded with guidance to help you to listen out for things, but that guidance becomes progressively less explicit until you no longer need it.

1

The final Chapters 8 to 12 on intonation are a thorough and comprehensive introduction to transcribing the important features of intonation.

There is a convention that when spoken discourse is transcribed it is done so in ordinary orthography; and this convention is accepted here. It should be noted that much of the spoken data in sociolinguistics literature has very poor systems for recording intonation and its effect in the development of discourse, and these final chapters will gradually introduce you to the intonation systems themselves in real, genuine instances of talk that were recorded for other purposes than intonation transcription. Intonation is there whenever we talk, and it is often the most crucial element in the communication process. So you get to handle intonation in actual talk, not in simulated exercises.

These chapters could be taken as a separate task from the rest of this book. They present a full description of intonation, but they do so in such a way that you build up both your knowledge and your skill in transcription. There are occasional references to new trends which are not always dealt with in textbooks on English intonation. Again, there is an emphasis on intonation in *real* discourse; you will listen to real people talking in real situations, not in simulated exercises.

You will see that the exercises in Chapters 8 to 12 do not have a key. This is because you are introduced to real dialogues where you have to decide on matters of tonality first and then on matters of tonicity and then of tone and paratones. As you move from one chapter to another, the 'key' is given you in every following chapter. So, for example, you are asked to decide on the tonality of dialogues in Chapter 8 before you move on to tonicity in Chapter 9; and when you come to work on tonicity, you will find that the tonality of the dialogue is presented to you, because you cannot really decide on matters of tonicity until the tonality has been recognized. And so it goes on, step by step through to Chapter 12, until you have reached a full and complete analysis and transcription.

So you get the chance to learn and practise and then produce whole transcriptions with confidence, from simple words to whole discourses, all in one workbook!

I Words . . .

Why transcribe?

It is an unfortunate feature of the English language, that the way its words are spelt does not always match the way its words are pronounced, in the simple and systematic way of other languages. For instance, in most accents of English, the letter <a> is not pronounced the same in the two words *tall* and *tally*; and although the two words *tally* and *ally* are spelt alike, they are not pronounced alike – they do not rhyme. There are, in fact, two sides to this mismatching of spelling and pronunciation: a single vowel letter of the alphabet can represent at least two vowel sounds; and a single vowel sound can be represented by at least two different spellings. Another example is the double <o> in *brood* and *brook* – two different vowel sounds, but the same spelling; and *brood* (what birds do) and *brewed* (past tense of the verb *brew*) – two different spellings, but the same vowel sound. In fact, it is not too difficult to think of ten ways of pronouncing the use of the letter <a> in spelling, and ten ways of pronouncing each of the other vowel **letters**. Equally, it is not too difficult to think of ten ways of spelling most of the vowel **sounds**. This represents an enormous task for a child learning to read and write in English as their mother tongue, and similarly, a tricky task for those who learn English as an additional language.

This mismatching is found amongst consonants too. The letter <t> in *rat* and *ration* represent very different consonant sounds; double <s> occurs in both *pass* and *passion*, but whereas *passion* and *ration* rhyme, their identical 'sh' sound is spelt differently. Have you noticed that the first double <s> in the word *possess* is pronounced differently from its second double <s>, and that the second double <s> of the word *possession* is different again? The variation amongst consonant letters and consonant sounds is not as great and as mystifying as it is amongst vowel letters and sounds, but it certainly adds to the impression of an unhelpful, perhaps even an unnecessary, complication in the matching up of spelling and pronunciation of words in English. You know, too, that often consonant letters represent nothing in pronunciation, like the <b> in *debt*, the <c> in *muscle*, the <d> in *handkerchief*, etc. But there is also the case of a consonant sound not being spelt at all: if you compare the pronunciation of the beginning of the two words *youthful* and *useful*, you will notice that the 'y' sound is spelt with the letter <y> in the first word, but is not spelt at all in the second; compare *view* and *few* too, where the 'y' sound is spelt with the letter <i> in *view*, but not in *few*.

Thus it is no wonder that learners have problems with English spelling and with deducing the pronunciation of words from their written form. These problems persist into later life and even well-educated professional people make many mistakes. So it is also no wonder that professionals in education have sought to remedy the situation by various means, including proposals for spelling reform on the one hand, and special reading schemes like phonics and the phonographic method on the other. But what is needed is an understanding of the very pronunciation system of English itself which the spelling system obscures. This need is met in the application of linguistics, or, more precisely, in those parts of linguistics known as phonology and phonetics. Phonology refers to pronunciation as a system in itself – how many vowels there are in the spoken form of the language (not the five vowel letters), and how many consonants there are, where the sounds can occur in words, what combination of sounds are allowed, etc. Phonetics refers to the pronunciation of the sounds themselves – how they are made, how they differ, how they sound in different positions of a word and how they sound in different combinations, etc. And for the study of the pronunciation of words in English, an extra set of symbols is needed to extend the use of the letters of the alphabet.

The use of such phonetic symbols, as they are usually called, facilitates the representation of the pronunciation of any language, not just those which have a 'difficult' relationship with spelling like English, French, Irish, etc. Even if there is a good correspondence between pronunciation and spelling as in languages like Spanish, Welsh, Finnish, etc., an international set of symbols is helpful in comparing languages and learning them. As you make your way through this workbook, you will also see that detailed differences can be represented when transcribing different accents and colloquial styles.

The 'angle' brackets, <t>, enclose letters of the alphabet. Whole words in ordinary spelling which are used as examples are in *italics*. 'Slant' brackets, /t/, enclose phonetic symbols in broad transcription, i.e. phonemes; whole words in broad transcription are also enclosed in 'slant' brackets, e.g. /ræt/ *rat*. 'Square' brackets, [t], enclose phonetic symbols in narrow transcription, i.e. allophones (see Chapter 4).

Chapters 1 to 3 are based on a type of accent that used to be known as *Received Pronunciation*. But this term is no longer transparent in meaning, and so the more explicit label *Southern England Standard Pronunciation* (SESP) is used. It also used to be known as *BBC English*, but the BBC now has a much more open policy on accents even for their main newsreaders, and of course other channels may well use newsreaders who speak with the SESP. This accent is 'standard' simply in the observation that it is recognized as a form of pronunciation that is typically used by those who professionally engage in public speech, people like newsreaders. But a newsreader in Scotland is not likely to use SESP, but a Scottish standard of pronunciation; similarly newsreaders in

Wales, Ireland, USA, Canada, etc. are most likely to use standard pronunciations that are appropriate in their settings.

There is no intrinsic 'value' in SESP or, for that matter, in General American (GA). However, SESP is the standard form of pronunciation that is presented in most descriptions of English pronunciation published in UK, while GA is the standard form presented in USA. Therefore, for simple practical reasons, SESP has been chosen as a starting point, but with occasional comments on well-known variations in other accents.

1 Vowels

The vowels offer the greatest problem, so we will start there. The vowel system of English is relatively large. Latin had five vowels, hence the five vowel letters in our Roman alphabet; a modern form of Latin, Spanish, has also only five, Italian has seven, but English has at least twenty. Listen to the following English names and note that each has a different vowel sound:

1.1 Steve, Jim, Jen, Pat, Mark, John, George, Brook, Sue, Chuck, Bert, Jane, Joe, Di, Joy, Ian, Claire, Noor

That's eighteen different vowel sounds already; then add to those, the two vowel sounds in

> Howard,

and the vowels at the beginning of

> Fiona and Louise.

And so the relatively large size of the vowel system of English can begin to be appreciated. All these different vowel sounds can be used to distinguish ordinary words too of course, such as

1.2 peat, pit, pet, pat, part, pot, port, put, putt, pert, pout . . .

and thus they have a contrastive function. By virtue of this contrastive function, we can be sure that all these vowel sounds are distinct items, or units, in the phonology of English – that is, in English pronunciation as a system. And because they are distinct, linguists need to have a separate symbol for each of them.

The phonetic description of the vowel sounds – that is, the way they are pronounced – helps us to classify them all into groups. There are three important groupings: the short vowels, the long vowels, and the weak vowels. Each will be dealt with in turn, beginning with the six short vowels.

The short vowels

The 6 short vowels can be found in the following words:

1.3 lick, leg, lack, lock, look, luck

They have two main features: one is that they are, phonetically, shorter than the other vowels, as we shall see when we introduce the long vowels; the other is that they are, phonologically, never able to appear at the end of a word in English – they must always be followed by a consonant. So, by introducing the short vowels first, we shall also have to practise the use of some of the consonant symbols. Some of the letters of the alphabet function also as phonetic symbols, such as b, d, f, g, h, k, l, m, n, p, r, s, t, v, w, z – all with their common English values. (Note that /g/ represents the initial sound in *get*, not that of *gem*.)

The symbols we will use are all authorized by the IPA, the International Phonetic Association, and can be used to represent the sounds of any language in the world. But please note that you must write them as printed, e.g. as /f/, not *ſ* ; as /z/, not *ʓ* , etc.

Now, the first short vowel that we listed was in the word

1.4   lick

that vowel is represented by a symbol that looks like a small capital < I >; ***lick* is transcribed as**

l ɪ k

Notice that the <ck> at the end of the word represents a single sound, and so only a single phonetic symbol, /k/, is required. Transcribe all these words too that rhyme with *lick* making sure that you write a /k/ all by itself at the end:

1.5   pick, tick, kick, nick, wick, trick, slick, stick

Write them on the line below

_____

One of these words could have been a name –

1.6   Nick

The name *Nick*, and the common noun, *nick*, are pronounced in exactly the same way despite the use of the capital <N>; because they are pronounced the same, they must be transcribed the same: /n ɪ k/. It would be phonetically incorrect to use a capital letter in a name as a phonetic symbol in a case like this. Notice also that the name, Nick, could also be spelt *Nic* or *Nik*, but because this makes no difference to the pronunciation, it makes no difference to the transcription either. So, *nick, Nick, Nic* and *Nik* are all transcribed as /n ɪ k/. (Because they are pronounced the same, despite their different spellings, the words are called homophones.)

Now, transcribe these other names, making sure you do not use any capital letters as phonetic symbols

1.7   Mick, Dick, Rick, Vic, Tim, Phil

_____

Here are some more words with the same vowel sound, to give you practice with the symbol /ɪ/.

1.8   pip, bib, did, kid, gig, fit, trip, slit, film, trim

_____

And now try these

1.9   licks, sticks, kicks, tricks, wicks, slicks

_____

Notice that they rhyme with the following names with apostrophe <'s >:

1.10   Nick's, Dick's, Rick's, Vic's, Mick's

_____

The apostrophe must **not** be included in the transcription, because it is **not** pronounced. And notice, too, that

1.11   *Mick's* and *mix*

are homophones – they are pronounced the same, and so should be transcribed the same: /mɪks/. Transcribe

1.12   six, fix, mix _____

You could also now transcribe the word

1.13   quick

using only the symbols introduced so far: /kwɪk/. Try:

1.14   quip, quit, quid, quiz, quill, quilt, squint, liquid, quick fix

_____

You could also transcribe the word

1.15   knit

noting that the initial <k> is not pronounced and so is not transcribed: /nɪt/ (*knit* and *nit* are homophones). Transcribe the following words in which, in each case, a letter is silent

1.16   wrist, biscuit, snippet, ticket, wicket

_____

Remember that /k/ is used whatever the spelling for the /k/ sound; so, *click* is /klɪk/. Then transcribe

1.17   crick, cricket, crib, crypt, script, clips, victim

_____

1.18   Vic prints Nik's scripts _____

1.19   Kim nicks Philip's biscuits _____

1.20   Six miss Rick's film _____

In this practice with the first short vowel, we have also actually illustrated a number of rules of good transcriptional practice:

1 A unit of sound in the phonological system of a language (known technically as a phoneme) must be represented by a single symbol, whatever variations may occur in spelling; e.g. <k, c, ck, q(u)> and an element of <x> all represent the one English consonant phoneme /k/.

2 Capital letters are not used for English phonemes; since <n> and <N> (etc.) are pronounced identically, they must be represented by a single symbol, e.g. /n/.

3 Homophones – pairs (or sets) of words with the same pronunciation despite different spellings – must be transcribed with the same symbols, e.g. *Mick's, mix.*

4 The apostrophe must not be transcribed, since it is not pronounced: *Mick's* = /m ɪ k s/ ; *Philip's* = /f ɪ l ɪ p s/.

5 A single letter may represent two phonemes in transcription; each of those phonemes requires its own symbol; e.g. <x> (in *six*) = /ks/.

6 A double letter may represent a single phoneme; in transcription that single phoneme must be represented by a single symbol; e.g. <ss> in *miss* = /m ɪ s/ ; <pp> in *snippet* = /s n ɪ p ɪ t/.

7 A letter may be redundant as far as pronunciation is concerned: if a letter represents 'silence', it must not have a corresponding symbol in the transcription of a word, e.g. <w> in *wrist* = /r ɪ s t/.

8 Word spaces are retained as in orthography, even when there is no 'space', or silence, in pronunciation. Note that the phrase *snip it* is pronounced identically to the single word *snippet.* However, word spaces are preserved to aid reading: /snɪp ɪt/.

A few more rules will need to be added in due course.

✳

The second short vowel that we listed occurred in the word

1.21   leg

That vowel is represented by an IPA symbol that looks like the Greek letter <ε>, (epsilon). So *leg* is transcribed as

l ε g

Some dictionaries use the ordinary Roman letter <e>, because it has a more familiar look; however, in IPA, <e> represents the sound in the German word

1.22 Tee

and the French word *thé*, Italian *té*, Welsh *tê*; or in many an English accent a word like *lake*. That vowel sound is distinctly different from the vowel in *leg*. Compare another pair of words: the word *late* in many English accents is pronounced:

1.23 'late'

compared to *let*. So, for comparative purposes, when, for instance, comparing the vowels of English and another language, or the vowels of two different accents of English, we need to keep the ordinary Roman letter <e> as the IPA symbol for the /e/ sound, and rely on the Greek letter epsilon, <ɛ>, as the IPA symbol for the /ɛ/ sound. Thus, *egg* is /ɛg/.

Using the symbol /ɛ/, now transcribe

1.24 peg, beg, keg _____

and

1.25 pet, net, debt, well, tent, send, kept, crept, twelve

_____

and the names

1.26 Ben, Greg, Kent, Meg, Rex, Brett _____

The vowel sound /ɛ/ is spelt in various ways including <ea>. Transcribe

1.27 head, dead, dealt, meant _____

and the homophones

1.28 *bread* and *bred*, and *wrecks* and *Rex* _____

Ate, the past tense of *eat*, in a British accent is usually

1.29 /ɛt/

Now transcribe

1.30 *friend* and *said* _____

1.31 Fred kept twelve tents _____

1.32 Ted said ten; Ed meant twelve _____

1.33 Did Meg wed Denis _____

1.34 Meg kept Denis in debt _____

1.35 Did Tim edit Phil's film script _____

1.36 Ed will edit it _____

Now try the word *extent*, remembering not to use the <x> letter. The first <e> is either /ɛ/ or /ɪ/

1.37   /ɛ k s t ɛ n t/, or /ɪ k s t ɛ n t/

Now transcribe

1.38   expend, excel, excess, except, expect, extensive, expensive, excessive, expressive

How do you pronounce the word *exit*:

1.39   /ɛksɪt/, or /ɛgzɪt/?

British people seem to be equally divided, but note the <x> can represent either pronunciation. Which pronunciation occurs in the word

1.40   *exist*?

How would you transcribe it? Transcribe the following words, carefully noting how the <x> is pronounced.

1.41   excess, exempt, exhibit _____

Did you notice the different rhythm in the two words *exit* and *exist*? In the first, the first syllable is stronger: *EXit* (however the <x> is pronounced). In the second the second syllable is stronger: *exIST*. In transcriptions, there is a mark ' placed at the beginning of a syllable to indicate the stronger stress. Thus

/'ɛ k s ɪ t / (or /'ɛ g z ɪ t /)   /ɛ g'z ɪ s t /

We have already used words with two syllables, disyllabic words, to illustrate the two short vowels /ɪ/ and /ɛ/. We should now add the stress mark to each of them, e.g. *biscuit* =

1.42   /'bɪskɪt/

Add the stress mark to the phonetic transcription of

1.43   snippet, ticket, wicket, cricket, Philip _____

extent, expect, excess, except _____

and to the three-syllabled (trisyllabic) words

extensive, expensive, excessive, exhibit

Transcribe the following words, including stress

1.44   mystic, cryptic, wicked, quintet, sextet, septic, sceptic (or American: skeptic), tennis

1.45 chemist, celtic (two possibilities), dissent, dispel, distill

---

1.46 diskette, dissect, incense (two possible stress patterns)

1.47 dismissive, etiquette, sensitive, dyslexic, disincentive

---

Before we turn to the third short vowel, we can add four more rules to good transcription practice.

> 9 A letter may represent two (or more) quite distinct phonemes, each of which must be transcribed distinctively; e.g. <c> may represent /k/ as in *crib* (= /k r ɪ b/) or /s/ as in *cent* (= /s e n t/); <x> may represent /ks/ as in *except* (= /ɛ k 's ɛ p t/) or /gz/ as in *exempt* (= /ɛ g 'z ɛ m p t/).
>
> 10 Two words spelt identically but pronounced differently – these are called homographs – need to be transcribed differently; *Celtic, incense.*
>
> 11 Degrees of syllable strength need to be marked, especially in words of more than one syllable, polysyllabic words; *incense* (an aromatic substance) = /'ɪ n s ɛ n s/ and *incense* (to enrage) = /ɪ n's ɛ n s/.
>
> 12 Alternative pronunciations in a single accent must be respected and corresponding alternative transcriptions acknowledged: *exit* may be either /'ɛ k s ɪ t/ or /'ɛ g z ɪ t/; *exist* may be either /ɪ g'z ɪ s t/ or /ɛ g'z ɪ s t/.
>
> These 12 rules need to be remembered and applied in the rest of this course, but having established them, we can now move more quickly through the remaining list of short vowels.
>
> *

The third short vowel listed was in the word

1.48 lack

It is traditionally represented by an IPA symbol that looks like the Old English 'ash' letter /æ/ as if a letter <e> was joined to <a>. You draw it by starting with a reverse <c>; then loop back through the middle of it, and finish with an <e>.

Alternatively, you can use the printed form of the letter <a>, but be careful to distinguish it from the handwritten shape that looks like this: ɑ. This is important, because we are going to need the handwritten shape for the symbol of a different vowel. To draw the 'printed <a>', you start with the top and front of the letter, drawing a curved top and a straight line down; then from the bottom point you draw a circle in front.

Lack is transcribed either as

l æ k *or* **l a k**

You choose! The first one is traditional and is also handy to represent American accents; the second one represents most modern British accents, especially of the younger generation. By having both symbols available, you can begin to see how we can exploit them for transcribing different accents. Get used to using one of them. You can then transcribe

1.49   pack, back, mac, knack, whack, quack, stack, track

_____

and also

1.50   cap, stab, flat, pram, lamb, ant, mass, tramp, axe, plaits

_____

Try

1.51   packet, acid, traffic, graphic, access, active (remember the stress mark!)

_____

and the names

1.52   Ann(e), Dan, Pat, Zac, Pam, Stan, Sam, Alice, Annette, Patrick

_____

And now this **k w ɪ k t ɛ s t**   **(1)**

1.53   pick   peck   pack _____

1.54   sit   set   sat _____

1.55   tin   ten   tan _____

1.56   sinned   send   sand _____

1.57   trick   trek   track _____   *(See Key)*

✳

The fourth short vowel in the list was in the word

1.58   lock

In British accents this vowel is represented by an IPA symbol that looks like a handwritten <a> upside down: /ɒ/. To draw it start with the hook at the top left; then drop down vertically and return with a curve to the right, up and round to the original hook.

The word *lock* is transcribed as

l ɒ k

You can then transcribe

1.59   dock, mock, knock, sock, rock, crock, flock, clock

_____

and also

1.60   pop, blob, trot, odd, clog, pomp, bond, off, moss, ox

_____

and

1.61   pocket, toxic, horrid, wedlock, con trick (with stress marks!)

_____

and the names

1.62   Tom, Don, Dot, Ron, Scott

_____

Notice these words that all have the vowel sound /ɒ/ despite their spelling with the letter <a>: *what is*

1.63   /wɒt/

Transcribe

1.64   want, wasp, swan, swamp, quad, squad, quadratic, squalid

_____

This short vowel /ɒ/ does not feature in most American accents; their alternative vowel sounds are dealt with in due course. However, the American speaker in Chapter 5 does use /ɒ/ in the words *lock* and *coffee*.)

★

The fifth short vowel in the list was in the word

1.65   look

The IPA symbol that represents this sound as it typically occurs in most accents of England and Wales looks like the Greek letter 'omega', but upside down: /ʊ/. You can draw this by starting with a hook at the top left and then descend and rise with a u-shape, finishing with a hook at the top right.

The word *look* is transcribed as

l ʊ k

You can then transcribe

1.66   took, book, cook, nook, hook, brook, stook

_____

and also

1.67   foot, good, soot, put, pull, bull, full, wood/would, could

_____

*

And finally, the sixth short vowel in the list was in the word

1.68   luck

The IPA symbol for this vowel looks like an upside down <v>: /ʌ/.
The word *luck* is transcribed as

l ʌ k

You can then transcribe

1.69   buck, duck, tuck, muck, ruck, truck, pluck

_____

and also

1.70   pup, cub, strut, slug, dumb, fund, sulk, slump, drum, crumb, struck

_____

and these names

1.71   Gus, Huck _____ _____

and then

1.72   monk, blood, flood, dove, come, love, front

_____

And then these homophones

1.73   sun / son   ____
       sum / some   ____
       plum / plumb ____

Can *you* distinguish between

1.74   *look, luck; took, tuck; rook, ruck; book, buck?*

If not, it might be because you speak with a British Midlands or Northern accent, which does not distinguish between these pairs of words! You might not have the /ʌ/ vowel in your accent at all! (See Chapter 5 for more evidence!) You will need to be careful and make this distinction if you are transcribing most other accents.

The word *one* is pronounced as either

1.75   /wʌn/ or /wɒn/

– or even /wʊn/ in some Northern accents. Check your own pronunciation and transcribe: *someone* _____. And

1.76   summit, pundit, uphill, uphold, upset (two stress possibilities, either as a noun (*an upset*) or a verb (*to upset*))

_____

1.77   undone, undress, unfit, unhook, unlock, unrest, unsaid, unstuck, unwell, unzip

_____

*

And another **k w ɪ k   t ɛ s t** (2)

1.78   pit   pet   pat   pot   put   putt   __ __ __ __ __ __
1.79   stick   stack   stock   stuck   ___ __ __ __
1.80   hit   hat   hot   hut   ___ __ __ __
1.81   hack   hock   hook   Huck   ___ __ __ __
1.82   hid   head   had   hod   hood   __ __ __ __ __
1.83   tick   Tec   tack   tock   took   tuck   __ __ __ __ __ __
1.84   slip   slap   slop   ___ __ __
1.85   rick   wreck   rack   rock   rook   ruck   __ __ __ __ __

(See Key)

*

The long vowels

The long vowels are – literally – longer than the short vowels. You might be able to hear the difference in the length of the vowels in the two words *grin* and *green*. If I am asked to say the vowel that occurs in *grin*, I am likely to say it as /ɪ/; and if asked to say the vowel in *green*, I am likely to say it as 'ee'. Now, if you can, compare the two together:

1.86 /ɪ/ ~ 'ee'

If you consult phoneticians' books on the description of English pronunciation, you will find details of this difference in length (see for instance Gimson 2008, Roach 2009, etc.). The long vowels are roughly twice the length of the short vowels; this is such a significant phonetic difference that it is the basis of one important grouping of vowels in English: long vowels distinct from short vowels.

There is also a phonological difference between the two: whereas short vowels have to be followed by a consonant in English, this is not the case for the long vowels – they can occur at the end of a word 'unchecked', as it were. The vowel in *green* appears at the end of the word *agree*, without the necessity of a consonant following. (A consonant *may* follow, of course, as in *agreed*, but it is not required as in the case of short vowels.)

Long vowels are themselves divided into two groups according to how steady the tongue is while they are being pronounced. If the tongue is relatively steady, they are called monophthongs (or 'pure' vowels); if there is a degree of movement by the tongue, they are called diphthongs. In my pronunciation of the 'ee' vowel, the tongue remains relatively stable, but when I pronounce the vowel *I* (or *eye*, or *aye*), the tongue rises to a higher position in the mouth and thus it qualifies as a diphthong. Said slowly, the movement of the tongue can be heard more easily:

1.87 "aayyee"

The length of the monophthongal long vowels is symbolised in the IPA by two points rather like a colon after the vowel symbol; for instance, the vowel in *green* is /iː/. The length of the diphthongal long vowels is symbolized by a double vowel symbol in which the starting and ending points of the tongue's movement are represented; for instance, the vowel in *I (eye, aye)* is transcribed as /aɪ/, where the /a/ represents the position of the tongue before it begins to move, and the /ɪ/ its position when it finishes.

It is important to think of the diphthongs as an essential part of a single vowel system in English, and not as a separate system. When languages and accents are compared, it may be tempting to treat the monophthongs and diphthongs separately, for convenience; but to do so would be highly misleading, as the short vowels and the long vowels – both monophthongs and diphthongs – form a *single* system. In fact, what is a diphthong in one accent may correspond to a monophthong in another, and vice versa, as we shall see in Chapter 5. And what is a monophthong in one language may have a diphthong as its nearest equivalent in another – and vice versa.

We will present the five monophthongal long vowels first because they can each be compared with a short vowel.

Monophthongs ('pure' vowels)

The vowel in

1.88   *green*

is a monophthongal long vowel. In most educated, standard, accents of English – not only in UK, but also around the world – this vowel requires a relatively steady tongue position. That position is close to the position the tongue has for the /ɪ/ vowel; hence, the sense of comparison between the two vowels. However, you can feel that the tongue position is slightly different; in the *green* vowel, the tongue is slightly higher, closer to the roof of the mouth, and slightly further forward, than it is for the *grin* vowel. (The *grin* vowel is then said to be lower, or opener, than the *green* vowel.) Because the tongue positions are different for the two vowels, the sound quality of the two is different; the difference in the sound quality is indicated in the IPA by a different shape to the symbol: /i/ represents the higher, closer, quality, whereas the /ɪ/ represents a slightly lower, opener, quality. Adding the length symbol gives us the symbol /iː/ for the *green* vowel; the whole word is thus transcribed as

g r iː n

Now transcribe

1.89   keen, mean, teen, dean, deem, lean, preen, dream

_____

and the homophones

1.90   sea / see   ____
       bean / been   ____
       leak / leek   ____
       team / teem   ____
       seam / seem   ____
       scene / seen   ____
       be / bee   ____
       meat / meet / mete   ____

and the names

1.91   Pete, Steve   ____   ____

Notice these spellings of the /iː/ vowel, and transcribe the words

1.92   ie   grief   ____
      ey   key   ____
      ay   quay   ____   (in British English)
      ei   deceive   ____

Compare and transcribe

1.93 seek sick ____ ____
      seat sit ____ ____
      peep pip ____ ____
      deed did ____ ____

Take your time to transcribe

1.94 antique _____

The second monophthongal long vowel is found in the word

1.95 palm

and is often compared to the short vowel of *Pam*. The *palm* vowel is not only longer but also – at least, in the case of most standard accents of UK and North America – it has a different sound quality. The tongue positions of the *Pam* and *palm* vowels are different; the tongue is positioned further back in the mouth for *palm*. This means that since the quality as well as the quantity is different, a different shape for the vowel symbol is required. The IPA uses the handwritten shape of <ɑ>, and, then, of course, the length symbol: /ɑː/. *Palm* is transcribed as

p ɑː m

The <l> in *palm* is, of course, not pronounced.
    Transcribe also

1.96 balm, calm, half, calf ____ ____ ____ ____

For most English-speaking people in England (but not necessarily the West Country), Wales, South Africa, Australia and New Zealand, the <r> in

1.97 park

is not pronounced either (these accents are called non-rhotic); this is, of course, not the case in Scotland, Ireland or most parts of North America, or for many people in the West Country of England (these, on the other hand, are called rhotic accents). The typical educated, standard, pronunciation in England for *park* is /pɑːk/. Transcribe the following words in this way, without a symbol for <r>:

1.98 lark, start, harm, farm, yard, smart

_____

and the names

1.99 Bart, Mark, Clark ____ ____ ____

Note and transcribe the homophones:

1.100 hart / heart ____
       bark / barque ____

Compare and transcribe

1.101   lark   lack   ____ ____

        stark   stack   ____ ____

        park   pack   ____ ____

        Bart   bat   ____ ____

        psalm   Sam   ____ ____

        barn   ban   ____ ____

1.102   carp   cap   ____ ____

        bard   bad   ____ ____

        can't   cant   ____ ____

Take your time to transcribe

1.103   art, artist, artiste, artistic, Arctic, Tarquin

———————————————————————————

Finally, there is another issue with the pronunciation of this vowel. How do you pronounce the word *class*? You will know of the rough division between SESP and others in this respect; Northerners use the /æ/ (/a/) vowel, whereas Southerners use the /ɑː/:

1.104   /klæs ~ klɑːs/

This choice of vowel is typically found before /-s, st, sp, f, ft, nt, ns/. Transcribe the following words in both types of pronunciation:

1.105   pass, grass, laugh, raft, plant, dance, last, grasp, graph

———————————————————————————

———————————————————————————

But notice that the following words are pronounced by the majority of Southerners with /æ/ (/a/), just like Northerners! Listen and transcribe:

1.106   ass, mass, crass, plastic, drastic, transfix

———————————————————————————

⋆

The third monophthongal long vowel occurs in the word

1.107   caught

and is often compared to the short vowel /ɒ/. The IPA symbol for the vowel in *caught* looks like a backward <c>; it represents a tongue position slightly higher, or closer to the roof of the mouth, than for /ɒ/. The IPA length mark is added: /ɔː/. Thus, the word *caught* is transcribed as

k ɔː t

And now transcribe

1.108   taught, fraught, haul, flaunt, raw, law, saw, prawn

_____

And notice these other spellings, and transcribe the words

1.109   <ou>   bought, brought, sought, ought, nought

_____

1.110   <oa>   broad _____

1.111   <a>   all, tall, small, fall   _____   _____   _____   _____

In these words, notice that the <l> is not pronounced:

1.112   talk, walk, stalk

_____

Many American accents have in fact an open long vowel /ɒː/ for all these words, but /ɔː/ only in words like *cork*

1.113   /kɔːrk/

However, the <r> is not pronounced in standard non-rhotic accents. Thus *cork* in SESP is transcribed as

k ɔː k

Transcribe these words

1.114   pork, port, snort, door, lord, corn, storm, store, more

_____

and these words with <ar> after <w> or <qu>

1.115   ward, warn, swarm, dwarf, quart, quartet

_____

Transcribe these names

1.116   Paul, Saul, Dawn, Maud

_____

and these homophones

1.117   awe / or / ore / oar   _____
        hall / haul   _____
        saw / sore   _____
        paw / pore / pour   _____
        law / lore   _____

caw / core   _____
flaw / floor   _____
caught / court   _____
taught / taut   _____
fought / fort   _____
sought / sort   _____
morn / mourn   _____
hoard / horde   _____

And then compare and transcribe the following pairs of words

1.118   taught tot   _____   _____
       wrought rot   _____   _____
       hawk hock   _____   _____

1.119   sport spot   _____   _____
       sworn swan   _____   _____
       Dawn Don   _____   _____
       Morse moss   _____   _____

Finally, a noticeable change is taking place in certain words involving the two vowels /ɔː/ and /ɒ/. Words with <al> or <aul> before <s> or <t> have both a conservative and a more modern pronunciation. Take the word *false*, for instance; you will hear both

1.120   /fɔːls/ and /fɒls/ ; and for *fault*, both /fɔːlt/ and /fɒlt/.

Transcribe these words in both pronunciations

1.121   halt, salt, vault, Walt, waltz, Austin

Take time to transcribe

1.122   morbid, uproar, caustic   _____   _____   _____

*

The fourth monophthongal long vowel occurs in the name

1.123   Luke

and is often compared to the short vowel /ʊ/ as in *look*. It is longer and the tongue position is slightly higher, or closer to the roof of the mouth. The IPA symbol is the letter <u>; added to it is the symbol for length : /uː/. Thus, *Luke* is transcribed

l uː k

The vowel of the word *food* is the same:

1.124   /fuːd/

Now transcribe

1.125 boot, hoot, moon, noon, soon, spoon, school, drool, cool

_____

1.126 tomb, womb, combe ____ ____ ____

1.127 and with <ue> true, clue, glue ____ ____ ____

1.128 and with <ew> brew, grew, crew ____ ____ ____

1.129 and with <ou> coup, soup, ghoul ____ ____ ____

and the homophones

1.130 loot / lute ____
blue / blew ____
flu / flue / flew ____
to / too / two ____

and the names

1.131 Sue, Trude, Andrew ____ ____ ____

There are very few pairs of words in English that contrast /uː/ with /ʊ/. Compare these and transcribe

1.132 pool pull ____ ____
fool full ____ ____
suit soot ____ ____
cooed could ____ ____
wooed would ____ ____

Take time to transcribe

1.133 lucid ____

*

The fifth monophthongal long vowel occurs in non-rhotic accents in the word

1.134 burn

and is often compared to the short vowel /ʌ/ as in *bun*. It is longer and the tongue position is slightly higher, or closer to the roof of the mouth. The IPA symbol is a reverse Greek <ɛ> (epsilon); the length symbol is added to it: /ɜː/. Thus *burn*, in non-rhotic accents, is transcribed

b ɜː n

The vowel /ɜː/ is associated mainly with spellings with <r> and thus rhotic accents do not have this vowel. Scottish speakers, for instance, use a variety of short vowels + /r/ (listen to the Scottish speaker in Chapter 5). But speakers of other rhotic accents often use a short form of /ɜː/ + /r/ as /ɜr/.

Other words with <ur> can now be transcribed

1.135   nurse, curt, spurt, turn, spurn, burst

_____

And now transcribe these words with <ir>

1.136   dirt, first, firm, squirm, squirt, quirk _____

1.137   with <er>:   verse, pert   _____

1.138   with <ear>:   learn, pearl   _____

1.139   with <wor>:   word, work, worm, world, worse   _____

and these homophones

1.140   fir / fur   ____
        berth / birth   ____
        herd / heard   ____
        kerb / curb   ____
        serf / surf   ____
        urn / earn   ____

Compare and transcribe

1.141   burn   bun   ____   ____
        fern   fun   ____   ____
        bird   bud   ____   ____
        curt   cut   ____   ____
        turn   ton   ____   ____

*

And now another **k w ɪ k t ɛ s t (3)** of all five long vowels

1.142   key, car, core, coup, cur   _____

1.143   teen, tarn, torn, tomb, turn   _____

1.144   speak, spark, sport, spook, spurt _____

1.145   keep, carp, cork, coop, curve   _____   *(See Key)*

*

And a **k w ɪ k t ɛ s t (4)** of all eleven vowels practised so far

1.146   peat, pit, pet, pat, part, pot, port, put, poop, putt, pert

_____

1.147   leak, lick, leg, lack, lark, lock, lawn, look, Luke, luck, lurk

_____

1.148 meek, Mick, Meg, mac, mark, mock, morn, nook, moon, muck, murk

---

Take time to transcribe

1.149 expert	1.150 advert	1.151 routine	1.152 placid
1.153 squalid	1.154 morphine	1.155 blackbird	1.156 seasick
1.157 service	1.158 plaudits	1.159 whirlpool	1.160 heartburn
1.161 clockwork	1.162 stopgap	1.163 girlfriend	1.164 workforce
1.165 football team		1.166 fun park	*(See Key)*

*

Diphthongs

The diphthongs are long vowels – as has already been explained – in which there is a noticeable movement of the tongue. In English the movement of the tongue has three possible directions: either higher towards the front of the roof of the mouth, that is, in the general direction towards the /ɪ/ or /iː/ vowel; or higher towards the back, that is, in the general direction towards the /ʊ/ or /uː/ vowel; or towards a central area, that is, in the general direction of the /ʌ/ or /ɜː/ vowel. These three directions are called front closing, back closing and centring, respectively.

There are three 'front closing' diphthongs in Southern English Standard Pronunciation; they occur in the following words and name:

1.167 lake, like, Lloyd

In the first one, *lake*, the tongue does not move a great deal, but you can nevertheless feel the movement as you imitate the vowel sound by itself 'a. . . .e'. Its symbol is a double one, indicating the positions of the tongue at the beginning and at the end of the movement: /eɪ/. The [e] indicates a tongue position a little closer than the English /ɛ/ and more like the vowel in the German word *Tee* (French *thé*, etc.). And the second part [ɪ] indicates the position of the tongue at the end of the diphthongal movement.

Say the vowel slowly, to give yourself time to feel the movement of the tongue:

1.168 [eeeɪɪ]

Thus,

1.169 lake

is transcribed

l e ɪ k

You can now transcribe

1.170 bake, take, cake, make, sake, hake, wake, rake

_____

And the following words spelt with <ay>

1.171 pay, day, gay, hay, lay, stray

_____

And these with <ai>

1.172 aim, paid, main, rail, saint, quaint

_____

And the word

1.173 eight _____

Now these homophones

1.174 way / whey / weigh   _____
       wait / weight   _____
       strait / straight   _____
       tail / tale   _____
       grate / great   _____
       brake / break   _____
       stake / steak   _____
       Wales / whales / wails   _____

Transcribe these names

1.175 May, Mavis, David, Ray

_____

In the North of England, Scotland and Wales, an alternative standard pronunciation is heard, in which there is no diphthongal movement at all, but a long monophthong – just like the vowel in the German word *Tee*, French *thé*, etc. (Look back at pp. 9–10.) This vowel would be transcribed as /eː/. Listen to it in the following few examples:

1.176 lake   bake   take   great/grate brake/break stake/steak Wales/whales

       /leːk/ /beːk/ /teːk/ /greːt/   /breːk/   /steːk/   /weːlz/

This alternative is taken up again in Chapter 5.

*

The second front closing diphthong appears in the word

26

1.177 like

The symbol has already been mentioned on p. 17: /aɪ/, which indicates a beginning position of the tongue like the /a/ and an ending like /ɪ/. Say the word *I / eye / aye* in slow motion again:

1.178 /aaaɪɪ/

Thus *like* is transcribed

l aɪ k

The homophones *I, eye, aye* are transcribed simply as /aɪ/.
Now you can transcribe

1.179 pike, bike, wipe, bite, wide, rhyme, nice

_____

and these

1.180 lie, tie, die, pie, my, sty, cry, why, spry

_____

and these with <igh>

1.181 high, light, bright, might, plight, height, tight

_____

and these homophones

1.182   rite / write / right / wright   _____
  die / dye   _____
  rye / wry   _____
  by / buy / bye   _____
  stile / style   _____
  white / Wight   _____
  dike / dyke   _____
  night / knight   _____

And these names

1.183 Mike, Di, Diane, Clive _____

*

The third front closing diphthong occurs in the name

1.184 Lloyd

In this case, not only does the tongue move, but the lips change shape too. The tongue moves from the position for the /ɔː/ vowel to the position for the /ɪ/. Thus, the symbol is /ɔɪ/ and *Lloyd* is transcribed

l ɔɪ d

You can now transcribe

1.185 void, voice, noise, coin, quoit _____

and these words with <oy>

1.186 boy, coy, ploy, toy _____

and these names

1.187 Boyd, Roy, Troy _____

⋆

And another **k w ɪ k   t ɛ s t (5)**

1.188 ale   isle   oil   ___ ___ ___

1.189 bay   by/buy   boy   ___ ___ ___

1.190 Kate   kite   quoit   ___ ___ ___

1.191 tray   try   Troy   ___ ___ ___

1.192 paint   pint   point   ___ ___ ___   *(See Key)*

⋆

There are just two 'back closing' diphthongs: they occur in the words *load* and *loud*.

The first one, as in

1.193 load

has a number of variations, but the main one in Southern English Standard Pronunciation has the tongue beginning in a central position and finishing like /ʊ/ or /uː/. The IPA symbol for the initial position of the tongue is like an upturned, inverted <e>: [ə]; this symbol is called *schwa*. To draw it, you start from the top left point, draw a reverse <c> symbol, and then loop back to the middle.

The whole symbol is /əʊ/. *Load* is thus transcribed as

l əʊ d

Now you can transcribe

1.194 toad, oats, boat, goat, float, gloat, bloat, roam

and the words

1.195 go, foe, low, slow, snow, grow

_____

and the words

1.196 own, stone, bone, poke, rogue, stove, stroke, comb

_____

Now the homophones

1.197 rode / road   _____
      know / no   _____
      broach / brooch   _____
      toe / tow   _____
      doe / dough   _____
      lone / loan   _____
      Flo / flow   _____

North American accents generally render this diphthong as /oʊ/ since the tongue moves from a back position. But there is also an important variation to the /əʊ/ vowel in Southern English Standard Pronunciation, before the consonant /l/. In this case, the tongue begins in the position for the /ɒ/ vowel, and moves to /ʊ/. Listen to the two pronunciations of the word *old*: the standard

1.198 /əʊld/ and the alternative /ɒʊld/.

This variation in the pronunciation of the vowel occurs only before the consonant /l/ in the same syllable. Transcribe the two versions of the following words

1.199 cold, bolt, toll _____

and the homophones

1.200 hole / whole   ____ ____
      role / roll   ____ ____
      sole / soul   ____ ____

In addition to this variation in SESP, a quite different sound to this vowel is heard in Northern English, Scottish and Welsh standard pronunciations and sounds like the long monophthong in the French word *chaud* ('hot'), German *so*, Welsh *lôn*. It is transcribed in IPA as the letter <o> with length marks: /oː/. Listen to the following few examples

1.201 load   go   stone   comb   stroke
      /loːd/ /goː/ /stoːn/ /koːm/ /stroːk/

This will also be referred to again in Chapter 5.

＊

The other back closing diphthong, as in

1.202 loud

has a tongue movement which begins close to the beginning of /aɪ/ but moves in the direction of /ʊ/ or /uː/. Thus its symbol is /aʊ/ and *loud* is transcribed as

l aʊ d

In some descriptions, the <ɑ> letter shape is used instead, but in practical terms, this makes very little difference in English.

Now transcribe

1.203 proud, cloud, crowd, scout, sprout, house, found, count

_____

and these words

1.204 how, now, brown, cow _____

Notice the two pronunciations of these homographs, which rhyme either with

1.205 *prow*

or with

1.206 *crow*

Transcribe the two possibilities

1.207 row ____ ____
       bow ____ ____
       sow ____ ____

*

Another **k w ɪ k t ɛ s t (6)**

1.208 now   no/know ____ ____

1.209 town   tone   ____ ____

1.210 stout stoat   ____ ____

1.211 found phoned   feigned find ____ ____ ____ ____

1.212 fowl   foal   fail   file foil ____ ____ ____ ____ ____

(See Key)

*

Finally, the three 'centring' diphthongs which appear in the words *leer, lair* and *moor*. In the first case, the tongue begins near the /ɪ/ or /iː/ position and moves to the central area; the symbol is a combination of /ɪ/ and schwa: /ɪə/. Thus,

1.213 leer

is transcribed

l ɪə

And now you can transcribe

1.214 ear, gear, near, rear, mere, sneer, queer, beard

_____

and the homophones

1.215 peer / pier   ____
       beer / bier   ____
       deer/ dear   ____
       here / hear   ____

The word *year* has two pronunciations; listen and transcribe them both

1.216 year ____   ____

Transcribe the names

1.217 Nia, Ian / Iain ____   ____

You might sometimes hear some younger SESP speakers lose the tongue movement to /ə/ and produce the vowel as /ɪː/. Listen out for it!

*

The second centring diphthong, as in

1.218 lair

has the tongue in the position for the vowel /ɛ/ before it moves to the central area. The symbol is a combination of /ɛ/ and schwa: /ɛə/. Thus *lair* is transcribed

l ɛə

When we first introduced the short vowel /ɛ/, as in *leg*, we noted that some dictionaries employ the more familiar letter <e> of the Roman alphabet; those dictionaries also employ that letter in the transcription of this diphthong, as /eə/.

Using the Greek letter <ɛ> and *schwa* /ə/, transcribe

1.219 air, dare, care, rare, square, prayer _____

and the homophones

1.220 fair / fare   ____
       flair / flare   ____
       hair / hare   ____
       bear / bare   ____

31

wear / where   ____
mare / mayor   ____

and the two pronunciations of the homograph *tear*; transcribe them both

1.221   tear   ____   ____

You might note here another noticeable change in the pronunciation of centring diphthongs in SESP; in this case /ɛə/ is produced as a long monophthongal

1.222   /ɛ:/

This is now so widespread that within a generation it may well be accepted as the standard SESP form. Listen to the difference between the traditional diphthong and this modern variation in the word *lair*

1.223   /lɛə/, /lɛ:/

Here are some more examples; transcribe them in both ways

1.224   dare, square, care   ____   ____   ____

____   ____   ____

and the name Clare / Claire in both ways   ____   ____

Compare and transcribe these pairs of words:

1.225   pear pier   ____   ____
stair steer   ____   ____
bear beer   ____   ____
hair hear   ____   ____
fare fear   ____   ____

*

The third centring diphthong, as in

1.226   moor

has the tongue in the position for /ʊ/, before it moves to the central area. The symbol is a combination of /ʊ/ and /ə/: /ʊə/. Thus, *moor* is transcribed

m ʊə

You can now transcribe

1.227   poor, tour, boor, dour   _____

However, here too there is a very strong tendency among the younger generation of SESP speakers to replace this diphthong entirely – mainly by substituting it with the long monophthong

1.228   /ɔ:/

Thus *moor* becomes homophonous with *more*, *poor* with *paw/pour/pore*, *tour* with *tore*, and *boor* with *bore*. Similarly the word *sure* is now much more commonly pronounced as homophonous with *shore,* rather than with the diphthong /ʊə/.

1.229 /mʊə, mɔː/ /pʊə, pɔː/ /tʊə, tɔː/ /bʊə, bɔː/ /ʃʊə, ʃɔː/

However, the alternative pronunciation of *dour* does not follow this pattern; it is not /dɔː/ ('*door*'), but /daʊə/ and produces a homophone with *dower.*

1.230 /dʊə, daʊə/

In rhotic accents, the centring diphthongs do not exist as such, since the final letter <r> is pronounced. In these accents the words *leer, lair* and *moor* are pronounced with an equivalent short vowel and a final /r/ as

1.231 /lɪr/, /lɛr/, /mʊr/

*

And a k w ɪ k t ɛ s t (7) on the centring diphthongs						
1.232	tier	tare	tour	____	____	____
1.233	mere	mayor	moor	____	____	____
1.234	spear	spare	spoor	____	____	____
1.235	speed	speared	sped	spared	____ ____ ____ ____		
1.236	bead	beard	bed	bared	____ ____ ____ ____		
1.237	feed	feared	fed	fared	____ ____ ____ ____ *(See Key)*		

*

The weak vowels

And, finally, the weak vowels. The weak vowels are confined to weak, unstressed, syllables. All the short and long vowels introduced already are all strong vowels and all occur in strong, stressed, syllables. The short vowels /ɪ/ and /ʊ/ can also occur in weak syllables, but there are three weak vowels in SESP which can occur in weak syllables only.

These three weak vowels resemble the three finishing points of the three kinds of English diphthongs; they are pronounced with the tongue in either a 'front close' position, a 'back close' position, or a 'central' position.

The first one occurs at the end of a word like

1.238 coffee

The final vowel is in an unstressed syllable, it does not usually have the length of the /iː/ vowel as in the word *fee*, and the tongue can vary between a position for the /iː/ vowel and the /ɪ/ vowel without any consequences for the meaning of the word. There is a certain variability about the actual pronunciation of these weak vowels, and this is reflected in a kind of compromise symbol – the letter <i>, but without the length marks: /i/. Thus *coffee* is transcribed as

33

'kɒfi

This weak vowel occurs in the following words too: listen and transcribe

1.239   city, valley, happy, quickly _____

and the names

1.240   Tony/Toni, Mary, Annie, Betty, Bobby, Sophie, Harry, Henry

_____

It also occurs in the middle of words before a vowel, as in

1.241   *audio* /'ɔːdiəʊ/

1.242   *video* /'vɪdiəʊ/

1.243   *mediate* /'miːdieɪt/

Thirdly, it occurs in the weak forms of words like *he, we, me, be,* that is, when these words are unstressed, e.g. *he likes me; we live in Wales; be quick*

1.244   /hi 'laɪks mi/

1.245   /wi 'lɪv ɪn 'weɪlz/

1.246   /bi 'kwɪk/

*

The second weak vowel occurs likewise in the middle of words before a vowel, as in

1.247   *(to) graduate* /'grædjueɪt/, *Louise* /luˈiːz/

It also occurs in the weak form of a word like *to* before a vowel, and at the end of a clause; the vowel is not usually as long as the vowel /uː/ and the tongue position varies between the /uː/ and /ʊ/ vowels; hence, its symbol is also a kind of compromise: the letter <u>, but without the length marks: /u/. Examples with unstressed *to* are *to act; to own; to everyone.*

1.248   /tu 'ækt/

1.249   /tu 'əʊn/

1.250   /tu 'ɛvriwʌn/

and in final position: *I want to; who will he talk to?*

1.251   /aɪ 'wɒnt tu/

1.252   /'huː wɪl i 'tɔːk tu/

You and *who* also have weak forms: /ju/ and /hu, u/; for example, *how d'you do?; thank you; who's there?; a man who can.*

1.253   /ˈhaʊ d ju ˈduː/; /ˈθæŋk ju/; /hu z ˈðɛə/; /ə ˈmæn u ˈkæn/

                                    ⋆

Last, but not least, the third weak vowel, which is in fact the commonest vowel in English pronunciation. It is produced with the tongue in a central position and sounds rather like a hesitation:

1.254   uh

It is often called the 'neutral vowel' because the tongue requires no muscular effort as it does to produce front and back vowels and close and open vowels; it is like 'neutral gear'. Its symbol is the schwa: /ə/, which was first introduced as the beginning of the back closing diphthong /əʊ/ and then as the end of all the centring diphthongs. Like the other weak vowels, it is confined (in Southern English Standard Pronunciation) to unstressed syllables, as in the final syllables of

1.255   farmer, drama

It is important to notice that in non-rhotic accents, the <r> at the end of *farmer* is not pronounced, and the two words *farmer* and *drama* rhyme. They are transcribed as

ˈfɑːmə ˈdrɑːmə

Transcribe these words, without a final /r/

1.256   better, driver, actor, doctor, harder, cider, licker / liquor

   _____

and these words

1.257   comma, sofa, vodka, pizza _____

and these names

1.258   Fiona, Emma, Rita, Sarah, Noah, Anna, Hannah, Peter, Robert, Rupert

   _____

The neutral vowel also occurs in the following suffixes

1.259   <-an>   African, Indian, Italian, Zambian
1.260   <-ous>   porous, parlous, raucous, serious
1.261   <-less>   helpless, fearless, hapless, careless
1.262   <-ness>   darkness, weakness, sadness, happiness

and in the following unstressed prefixes

1.263   <com->   combust, commence, commit, compare
1.264   <con->   conceal, condemn, confront, connect
1.265   <col/r->   collect, collide, collate, collapse, correct, corrode

1.266 <sub-> submit, subside, subscribe, subtract
1.267 <suc-> succeed, success, succumb
1.268 <sur-> surround, surmount, surreal, survive

It also occurs as the weak vowel represented by a variety of vowel letters in unstressed syllables: take for instance *banana*. The letter <a> occurs three times: once in the second syllable as a strong /ɑː/ in SESP or /æ/ in American accents, and twice as the weak vowel /ə/ in the two unstressed syllables.

1.269 banana

is transcribed as

bəˈnɑːnə / bəˈnænə

How would you transcribe

1.270 *Canada, Granada* and *Panama*?

——————————————————————

Transcribe the names

1.271 Amanda, Abraham, Clement, Reuben, Christopher, Raymond, Callum, Titus

——————————————————————

We have now covered the whole vowel system of English!

＊

See if you can transcribe these **place names (1)**

1.272	Aberdeen	1.277	Fulham	1.282	Liverpool
1.273	Cardiff	1.278	Glasgow	1.283	Leeds
1.274	Derby	1.279	Gloucester	1.284	Sunderland
1.275	Edinburgh	1.280	Hull	1.285	Swansea
1.276	Exeter	1.281	London	1.286	Worcester

(See Key)

＊

Summary

The total inventory in the vowel system of Southern English Standard pronunciation can be displayed in the following set of charts. The approximate position of the tongue for each vowel is shown by indicating relative frontness to the left, backness to the right, and relative closeness and openness on the vertical axis.

ɪ	ʊ
ɛ	
	ʌ
a/æ	ɒ

iː	uː	ɪə	ʊə
		eɪ	
ɜː		ɛə	əʊ
	ɔː		ɔɪ
ɑː		aɪ	aʊ

i	u
	ə

short vowels long vowels weak vowels

And now the consonants – but most of them have been introduced already!

2 Consonants

In most standard accents of English, there are twenty-four consonants, and they are grouped into five types: plosives, nasals, fricatives, affricates and approximants.

Plosives

Plosives are usually introduced first because the kind of constriction in the mouth by which they are produced is total. There are six of them: /p, b, t, d, k, g/

/p/ and /b/ are produced with the constriction at the lips (bilabial). In the case of /p/, the vocal folds (cords) produce no voicing, and so /p/ is consequently known as a voiceless plosive.

/t/ and /d/ are produced with the constriction of the blade of the tongue against the ridge behind the upper teeth (alveolar); /t/ is voiceless.

/k/ and /g/ are produced with the constriction of the back of the tongue against the back of the roof of the mouth, the soft palate (velar); /k/ is voiceless.

Transcribe these words

2.1 cap, cab ____ ____   peck, peg ____ ____
     rope, robe ____ ____   hake, Hague ____ ____
     debt, dead ____ ____   bright, bride ____ ____

2.2 croquet, league, grotesque, chemist, school, stomach, ache

---

Note that <p> is silent in *receipt* and many words like *psychology, pneumatic*.
<b> is silent in *debt, doubt, subtle* and in *lamb, tomb, climb, plumb*.
<t> is silent in *listen, whistle, soften, Christmas* and at the end of many words of French origin like *ballet*.
<d> is silent in *handsome, handkerchief, sandwich* and for most people also in *Wednesday*.
<k> is silent at the beginning of words before <n>: *knee, knife, knock*.
<g> is silent likewise: *gnat, gnome*; and at the end of words also: *sign, foreign*.

*

Nasals

Nasals have the same constriction as plosives except that air is allowed to pass through the nose, but not through the mouth. There are three nasals in English: /m/ (bilabial), /n/ (alveolar) and /ŋ/ (velar); none of them are voiceless. The IPA symbol for the velar nasal is the letter <n> supplemented with the tail of <g> as in the words

2.3   *bank* /bæŋk/, *anger* /ˈæŋgə/

and is also found as the <ng> spelling at the end of a word like *bang* /bæŋ/. The letter <g> is not pronounced separately in such words in SESP.
    Transcribe these words

2.4   ink, drink, prank, zonk, drunk, sprinkler, conquer, conquest
    _____

2.5   finger, stronger, singlet _____

2.6   spring, song, clang _____

Notice too the /ŋ/ in the suffixes *-ing* and *-ling*. Transcribe these words

2.7   eating, drinking, singing _____
    morning / mourning, evening _____

2.8   inkling, weakling, fatling _____

                                    *

Fricatives

Fricatives have a looser constriction in the mouth, which allows friction to be produced at the point of contact. There are nine fricatives: four pairs and /h/. /f/ and /v/ are produced with the constriction between the lower lip and the upper teeth (labiodental); /f/ is voiceless. Compare and transcribe

2.9   grief, grieve   ____ ____

2.10 safe, save   ____ ____

2.11 belief, believe   ____ ____

2.12 half, halve   ____ ____

2.13 proof, prove   ____ ____

A second pair of fricatives has the constriction between the tip or blade of the tongue and the upper teeth (dental); they are both spelt <th>. The two words *thin* and *then* illustrate the two; in

2.14 thin

the <th> represents a voiceless fricative, which has an IPA symbol that looks like the Greek letter theta <θ>; on the other hand, the <th> in

39

2.15 then

is voiced and this has an IPA symbol that looks like an old-fashioned <d> crossed with a stroke through it: /ð/. Compare the two and notice the difference in voicing:

2.16 /θ/, /ð/

The voiceless dental fricative /θ/ occurs typically at the beginning of nouns, verbs and adjectives. Listen and transcribe:

2.17 thin, thing, think, thinker, thought, thumb, three, thrive, thwart

_____

On the other hand, the voiced dental fricative /ð/ occurs at the beginning of the following grammatical words; listen and transcribe

2.18 then, this, that, these, those, there/their, theirs, they, them, thus, though

_____

Which kind of <th> occurs at the beginning of the word *through*? Transcribe it.

2.19 through   _____

The two <th>s occur in the middles of words, but it is noticeable how the voice-less dental fricative /θ/ features medially in words of Latin and Greek origin, whereas the voiced dental fricative /ð/ appears in words of Germanic origin. Compare the words

2.20 *author* /ˈɔːθə/, *other* /ˈʌðə/

2.21 *method* /ˈmɛθəd/, *mother* /ˈmʌðə/

Transcribe these words

2.22 ethics, pathos, anthem, ether _____

2.23 father, mother, brother, further, southern, northern, worthy

_____

Which kind of <th> occurs in your pronunciation of the word *earthen*? People vary: transcribe both possibilities:

2.24 earthen   _____   _____

The two <th>s also occur at the ends of words; the voiceless /θ/ usually occurs at the end of nouns and adjectives, whereas the voiced /ð/ occurs at the end of verbs and prepositions. Compare *teeth* and *to teethe*.

2.25 teeth, teethe

Transcribe

2.26   teeth, mouth, wreath, bath, breath, north, south, myth, health, worth

_____

2.27   fourth, fifth   ____   ____

2.28   teethe, (to) mouth, wreathe, bathe, breathe, writhe, soothe, with

_____

But notice that the words *lathe* and *scythe* are both nouns and verbs but are pronounced the same, and the word *smooth* is both an adjective and a verb. Which type of <th> do they all end with? Transcribe them

2.29   lathe, scythe, smooth   _____

The third pair of fricatives, /s/ and /z/, have the constriction between the blade of the tongue and the ridge behind the upper teeth (alveolar); /s/ is voiceless. Notice that the letter <c> often represents /s/; and the letter <s> often /z/!

Transcribe the following homophones

2.30	sent / scent / cent ____	2.31	freeze / frees ____
	sealing / ceiling ____		raise / raze / rays / Ray's ____
	seed / cede ____		daze / days ____
	sight / site / cite ____		maze / maize / May's ____
	dissent / descent ____		knows / nose ____
	practise / practice ____		cruise / crews ____

Notice the two pronunciations of the homographs *close* and *house*:

2.32   close

2.33   house

In each case, it is the verb that has /z/. Notice, too, the pair *loose* and *lose*, again, it is the verb that has /z/. Transcribe all three pairs

2.34   close   ____ ____
        house   ____ ____
        loose/lose ____ ____

Transcribe these words

2.35   scissors   2.36 possess   2.37 decent   2.38 deceit

2.39   licence/license   2.40 laser   2.41 scenic

2.42   physics   2.43 realise/realize   2.44 Leslie/Lesley

Note that <s> is silent in *island, isle, aisle, viscount* and at the end of many words of French origin: *corps, debris, precis*.

The fourth pair have the constriction between the body of the tongue and the forward part of the roof of the mouth, immediately behind the teeth ridge (post-alveolar; or traditionally, 'palato-alveolar'). The IPA symbol for the

41

voiceless post-alveolar fricative is like a letter <s> stretched high and low: /ʃ/; and is often represented by the letters <sh> in English – in fact, in the word

2.45   English

itself. The IPA symbol for the voiced post-alveolar fricative looks like a hand-written <z>; /ʒ/. It is, thus, important to keep the **printed** shape of the letter <z> for the sound /z/ and to reserve the handwritten shape for the /ʒ/ sound. These two new symbols are often called

2.46   *esh /ɛʃ/, zhed /ʒɛd/*

as reminders of the sounds they symbolize. Transcribe these words

2.47   ship, sheep, shoe, rush, cash, English

_____

2.48   sugar, machine, pressure, conscience, ocean, chic, chauffeur

_____

and the names

2.49   Sheila / Shelagh, Sharon, Cheryl, Michelle, Shaun / Sean

_____

Notice, too, that the suffixes *-tion* and *-ssion* are pronounced as /-ʃən/. Transcribe

2.50   nation, ration, passion, mission, function, constriction

_____

and the suffixes *-cial* and *-tial* with /-ʃəl/. Transcribe

2.51   special, crucial, financial, essential

_____

and similarly the suffixes *-cious* and *-xious* as /-ʃəs/

2.52   atrocious, conscious, precious, anxious, obnoxious

_____

Notice the /ʒ/ consonant in the middle of these words:

2.53   *casual /ˈkæʒʊəl/*

2.54   *pleasure /ˈplɛʒə/*

2.55   *vision /ˈvɪʒən/*

This is the least common consonant in English and is confined to the kind of contexts found in these words and in words of French origin. Transcribe

2.56 leisure, measure, treasure, visual

_____

2.57 division, derision, occasion, collision

_____

Notice, too, how people vary in their pronunciation of these words: *Asia* and *version*. Do you use /ʃ/ or /ʒ/? Transcribe the words in both ways

2.58 Asia, version _____ _____, _____ _____

And how about the word *transition*? Here the question is not only about /ʃ/ or /ʒ/, but about the pronunciation of the letter <s> as either /s/ or /z/. Listen to the four possibilities and try to transcribe each version

2.59 transition _____ _____ _____ _____

Certain French words have been borrowed into English. Listen and transcribe

2.60 genre, rouge, prestige, courgette, collage, montage, camouflage

_____

There are thus four pairs of fricatives; each pair has a voiceless fricative: /f, θ, s, ʃ/ and a voiced counterpart: /v, ð, z, ʒ/.

The ninth fricative is /h/, which is voiceless at the beginning of a word, but is usually voiced in the middle of a word; because the two voicing possibilities never contrast meanings of words in English, /h/ constitutes a single phoneme and so a single symbol is sufficient.

Transcribe the words

2.61 who, whom, whose, whooping cough _____

and the homophones

2.62 hole / whole   _____
      hoar / whore   _____
      holistic / wholistic _____

and these words

2.63 behave, behind, alcohol _____

Note that <h> is silent in

2.64 *hour, honest, honour, ghost, vehicle, vehement, annihilate*

Some Scottish, Irish and American speakers pronounce the <h> in other words beginning with <wh> besides those listed already; thus *whales* can be distinguished from *Wales*.

2.65 whales, Wales

The first word may then be pronounced as /hweɪlz/. Most people in England and Wales pronounce the two words as homophones: /weɪlz/. Transcribe the following words in the two ways and note the homophone possibilities.

2.66 what (watt)   ____ ____
      why (<Y>)   ____ ____
      when (wen)   ____ ____
      where (wear)   ____ ____
      whether (weather/wether) ____ ____
      while (wile)   ____ ____
      whine (wine)   ____ ____
      wheel (weal)   ____ ____
      whip   ____ ____
      white (Wight)   ____ ____
      whoosh   ____ ____

*

Affricates

An **affricate** consonant is a close knit sequence of plosive and fricative produced by a single organ of speech (articulator). In English, there are just two. One is commonly spelt <ch> and occurs, for instance, at the beginning of the word *chip*;

2.67 chip

Its IPA symbol is a combination of /t/ and /ʃ/ representing the sequence of plosive and fricative made by the body of the tongue in the post-alveolar area: /tʃ/. The symbol also indicates its voicelessness. The other affricate occurs at the beginning of the word *gem* and is commonly spelt with <g> (before <i> and <e>), <j>, and <dge>.

2.68 gem

Its IPA symbol is a 'voiced' equivalent of /tʃ/: a combination of /d/ for the plosive element and /ʒ/ for the fricative element: /dʒ/.

Chip is transcribed as

tʃ ɪ p

Compare and transcribe

2.69 chip, ship   ____ ____
      cheap, sheep   ____ ____
      cheek, chic   ____ ____
      catch, cash   ____ ____
      watch, wash   ____ ____
      porch, Porsche   ____ ____

Now transcribe

2.70 chill, child, church, such, bunch, belch

_____ _____

and the potential homophone

2.71 which/witch ____

and the name

2.72 Richard ____

/tʃ/ also occurs in the ending *-ture* as in

2.73 *venture* /ˈvɛntʃə /

Now transcribe

2.74 nature, stature, fracture, vulture, mature, picturesque

_____ _____

Gem is transcribed as

2.75 **dʒ ɛ m**

Now transcribe

2.76 gent, German, gist, ginger, giraffe, cringe _____

2.77 jump, pyjama/pajama, jubilee, rejoice, judge _____

2.78 edge, badge, bridge, fidget, bludgeon _____

The ending <-age> or <-ege> as in the words *village* and *college* is pronounced /-ɪdʒ/.

2.79 village, college

Transcribe

2.80 village, cabbage, haulage, message, wreckage, college, privilege

_____ _____

Compare these with loan words from French

2.81 college, collage   _____ _____
manage, montage   _____ _____
message, dressage   _____ _____
marriage, mirage   _____ _____
stoppage, sabotage   _____ _____
vestige, prestige   _____ _____

The two loan words, *garage* and *massage*, are becoming more anglicized in their pronunciation. Transcribe these variations of the two words

2.82   garage   _____   _____

       massage   _____   _____

Transcribe these names

2.83   George, Geoff/Jeff, Geoffrey/Jeffrey, Reg, Madge, Marjorie,

_____

2.84   Gemma, Gerald, Gerry/Jerry _____

2.85   John, Jean, Jim, Jack, James, Jemima _____

Compare and transcribe

2.86   edge, etch   _____   _____

2.87   badge, batch   _____   _____

2.88   surge, search   _____   _____

2.89   lunge, lunch   _____   _____

2.90   ledger, leisure   _____   _____

2.91   dredger, treasure   _____   _____

2.92   pigeon, vision   _____   _____

2.93   major, measure   _____   _____

*

A kwɪk tɛst (8) with the less familiar consonant symbols

2.94	think		sink	zinc	
2.95	ethics		Essex		
2.96	teeth	teethe		tease	
2.97	seethe	cease	seize		
2.98	sip	zip	ship		
2.99	seep		sheep	cheap	jeep
2.100	Mars	marsh	march	marge	
2.101	lease	Lee's	leash	leech	liege
2.102	Caesar		seizure		
2.103	composer		composure		
2.104	bays		beige		
2.105	ledger		leisure		
2.106	major		measure		

(See Key)

*

Approximants

There now remain just four **approximants**. An approximant is a consonant in which the constriction made by an organ of speech (articulator) is not great enough to produce any friction at all. The four approximants occur at the beginning of the words

2.107   *lot, rot, yacht* and *what*

The first is known as a **lateral approximant**, since the sides of the tongue are lowered while the blade presses against the upper teeth ridge (alveolar); this allows air to flow either side of the constriction without friction. It is typically spelt <l> or <ll> in English; its IPA symbol is /l/. *Lot* is transcribed as

l ɒ t

Linguists usually distinguish between two main varieties of /l/ in English: the *clear* /l/ that occurs before vowels and /j/ and the *dark* /l/, with the back of the tongue raised, that occurs before consonants (except /j/) or at the end of words. Since the two varieties never contrast meanings in English, together they constitute a single phoneme, and so only a single symbol is required. Transcribe

2.108   well, full, fulfil/fulfill, dollar _____

and the names:

2.109   Gill/Jill, Leo, Lionel, Billy, Sally _____

The *dark* /l/ seems to lead to an additional syllable when it occurs after the long monophthongs /iː/ and /uː/ and the diphthongs /eɪ, aɪ, ɔɪ, əʊ, aʊ/, that is when the tongue concludes the vowel articulation in a close, or high, position. The tongue needs time to adjust to the raising of the back of the tongue for the dark /l/, and this adjustment sounds like /ə/ and is known as **breaking**. As this adjustment is normal, and because no contrast in meaning is possible, there is no need to transcribe this breaking:

2.110   feel   fool   fail   file/phial   foil   foal   foul/fowl
        /fiːl/ /fuːl/ /feɪl/ /faɪl/   /fɔɪl/ /fəʊl/ /faʊl/

We take up the issue of breaking again in Chapter 4.

*

The second approximant is found at the beginning of *rot*.

2.111   rot

The blade (or, for some people, the front) of the tongue approaches (the back of) the teeth ridge (alveolar); its IPA symbol is an upturned <r>: [ɹ]; but for convenience, the ordinary letter <r> is used, except when English is being compared to another language. An <r> before a consonant or at the end of a word has been lost in pronunciation in the standard accents of England since the eighteenth century; these non-rhotic accents are now found also in Wales, South Africa, Australia and New Zealand. The rhotic accents of the West Country of England, Scotland, Ireland and North America retain a final /r/ in pronunciation, as we have already noted from time to time. *Rot* is transcribed

r ɒ t

Transcribe

2.112   raw, ready, rhyme/rime, rhetoric, lorry, quarry, carriage

_____

and the names

2.113   Ralph, Barry/Barrie, Lawrence, Laura, Sarah

_____

And now transcribe these words in both a rhotic and a non-rhotic accent

2.114   far, farm, chair, churn, shirt, journey

_____

_____

and these names in both a rhotic and a non-rhotic accent

2.115   Charles, George, Marjorie, Bart, Richard

_____

_____

*

The remaining two approximants are traditionally called semi-vowels because they are formed like close vowels, but they do not function as vowels. The approximant at the beginning of *yacht* is formed in a similar way to the /iː/ vowel; the body of the tongue is raised towards the roof of the mouth, the hard palate (palatal).

2.116   yacht

The IPA symbol is the letter <j>. Thus *yacht* is transcribed as

j ɒ t

Now you can transcribe

2.117   you, youth, young, yet, yeast, yellow, yearn

_____

The /j/ consonant also occurs in the spelling <ew, eu>. Notice that *you, ewe* and *yew* are homophones

2.118   /juː/

The word *few* is pronounced

2.119   /fjuː/

Now transcribe these words and include the /j/ symbol

2.120   feud, pew, view, queue/Kew _____

Note that in American accents no /j/ appears in such words after /t, d, n/; e.g. *dew, deuce, Tewkesbury, Tuesday, new, neuter*, whereas it does in British accents. And notice too that the following words with <ew> are no longer commonly pronounced with /j/

2.121   lewd /luːd/

2.122   chew /tʃuː/

2.123   Jew /dʒuː/

The /j/ consonant is not spelt directly in a word like *cute*.

2.124   cute

However, the /j/ consonant between the consonant /k/ and the vowel /uː/ must be transcribed, for the transcription /kuːt/ represents the word *coot*.

2.125   coot

The transcription of *cute* must include the /j/ symbol: /kjuːt/. Now transcribe

2.126   mute, music, unit, unite, union, consume, presume, beauty, futile

_____

and notice the two pronunciations of the homograph: *use*, and its derivatives *abuse, misuse*. In each case, the verb takes /-z/.

2.127   use, abuse, misuse

The difference between British and American accents with /d, t, n/ appears in these cases too: *due, tutor, nucleus*. Notice also that words with other alveolar consonants are no longer commonly pronounced with /j/, even in Britain:

2.128   rue, lute, flute, sue/Sue, suit

And finally, the approximant in the word *what*.

2.129   what

It is formed in a way similar to the vowel /uː/; the back of the tongue is raised towards the back of the roof of the mouth, the soft palate, while at the same time the lips are rounded and narrowed (labial-velar). The IPA symbol is the letter <w>; *what*, as you know already, is transcribed as

w ɒ t

The variation with <wh> words has already been practised, and we have also already noticed that the letter <w> is silent in the words *who, whole*, etc., and in *write, wreck, wreath, two*. It is also silent in the following words, so transcribe them without the /w/ symbol

2.130 wrong, wrought, wrap, wrath, wrench, wry, awry, answer, sword

---

*

Summary

We have now introduced all the consonants and the full inventory of them can be displayed in the following chart. In the case of voiceless and voiced pairs, the voiceless consonant appears on the left-hand side.

	Bilabial	Labio-dental	Dental	Alveolar	Post-alveolar	Palatal	Velar	Labial-velar	Glottal
Plosives	p b			t d			k g		
Nasals	m			n			ŋ		
Fricatives		f v	θ ð	s z	ʃ ʒ				h
Affricates					tʃ dʒ				
Lateral				l					
Approximants				r		j		w	

However, there are still two features of English pronunciation involving consonants that need explanation and practice: the occurrence of syllabic consonants and the form of consonants in inflections.

*

Syllabic Consonants

In certain circumstances in English, a consonant can constitute the centre (or peak) of a syllable instead of a vowel. It is clear that whereas a word like *sad* /sæd/ has one syllable, a word like *sadder* /ˈsædə/ has two. There is clearly a vowel articulated in the second, albeit unstressed, syllable after the consonant /d/. However, in words like

2.131 sadden, saddle

the matter is not so clear, because the consonant /d/ can be followed by either the consonants /n/ and /l/ without a vowel intervening. Listen to the two words in slow motion:

2.132   sadden, saddle

If you imitate these pronunciations, you should notice that the blade of the tongue maintains some kind of constriction as you proceed from the /d/ to the /n/ or /l/; there cannot possibly, therefore, have been a vowel in between!

In cases like these, the /n/ of *sadden* and the /l/ of *saddle* constitute the centre of the second, unstressed, syllable; this syllabic function of theirs is marked by a small mark [ˌ] below the consonant symbol. *Sadden* and *saddle* are transcribed thus:

ˈs æ d ņ   ˈs æ d ļ

Syllabic /n/ and /l/ typically occur in unstressed syllables immediately following the alveolar consonants, /t, s, z/ as well as /d/. Listen to, and transcribe, the following words

2.133   cotton _____   2.134   cattle   _____
        listen _____   whistle _____
        risen _____   drizzle _____

Syllabic /l/ can also follow /st/ or plain /n/ or /nt/

2.135   pistol, tunnel, mantle

_____

Transcribe these words

2.136   muddle, widen, smitten, hospital, loosen, hassle, cousin, weasel, gentle

_____

2.137   Bristol Channel

_____

and the names

2.138   Gordon, Jordan, Tarzan, Norton

_____

When the *-ing* suffix is added to a verb with a syllabic consonant, the syllabic consonant may either be retained as such or it simply becomes the initial consonant of the extra syllable. So, for instance, if *-ing* is added to the verb *listen*, the word becomes either a trisyllabic word with a syllabic consonant in the middle: *listening* /ˈlɪsņɪŋ/, or a disyllabic word: /ˈlɪsnɪŋ/. Listen to them again and compare them

2.139   /ˈlɪsņɪŋ/; /ˈlɪsnɪŋ/

Transcribe these words in the same two ways

2.140 whistling, drizzling, muddling, widening, loosening

_____

_____

But note that an intervening /ə/ occurs in

2.141 wanton, London, Hampton

_____

Notice that a syllabic /m/ often occurs in the word *happen* in colloquial speech as in

2.142 *If you want to make things happen* /ˈhæpm̩/.

And occasionally in the word *open*, as in

2.143 *None of them are open* /ˈəʊpm̩/.

With -*ing* added to these verbs, the /n/ is retained:

2.144 happening /ˈhæpnɪŋ/

2.145 opening /ˈəʊpnɪŋ/

In all these cases, the syllabic consonant follows immediately on a consonant made at the same point of articulation (homorganic articulation). Otherwise, the neutral vowel /ə/ intervenes as in, for example

2.146 *autumn* /ˈɔːtəm/

2.147 *bacon* /ˈbeɪkən/

2.148 *apple* /ˈæpəl/

Listen to, and transcribe, the following words with an intervening neutral vowel /ə/

2.149 table, soften, seven, southern, struggle, camel, cannon/canon, million, fashion, dungeon

_____

When the -*ing* suffix is added to a verb with the neutral vowel preceding the final consonant, the neutral vowel will often disappear. So, for instance, if -*ing* is added to the verb *soften*, the word becomes either /ˈsɒfənɪŋ/ with three syllables, or /ˈsɒfnɪŋ/ with two.

2.150 softening

Transcribe these words in these two ways

2.151 struggling, tackling, fashioning, beckoning, strengthening

_____

_____

The ending *-ism* is also pronounced with a neutral vowel between the /z/ and /m/; for instance

2.152 prism /'prɪzəm/

2.153 racism /'reɪsɪzəm/

2.154 feminism /'fɛmɪnɪzəm/

Also the word

2.155 chasm /'kæzəm/

Inflections

Inflections are endings that change the form of a word for a grammatical category without changing its grammatical class. Thus *sadder* and *saddest* contain inflections for the grammatical categories of *comparative* and *superlative* but the words remain adjectives, whereas the word *sadness* contains a derivational form that changes the word to the class *noun*.

The regular comparative inflection <-er> is pronounced /-ə/, or /-ər/ in rhotic accents; transcribe

2.156 deeper, fatter, higher, lower, quieter

_____

The regular superlative inflection <-est> is pronounced with either /-əst/ or /-ɪst/. Transcribe these words in both ways

2.157 deepest, fattest, highest, lowest, quietest

_____

_____

The regular past tense or past participle inflection <-ed> is pronounced in three different ways according to the final sound of the stem.

1 If the stem ends in the consonants /t, d/, the inflection is pronounced 'in full', either as /-əd/ or /-ɪd/, e.g.

2.158 *waited:* /'weɪtəd, 'weɪtɪd/; *added* /'ædəd, 'ædɪd/

(Can you detect which one *you* use?)

2 If the stem ends in a vowel or a voiced consonant (other than /d/), the inflection is pronounced in a reduced form /-d /, e.g.

2.159 *freed* /friːd/, *cried* /kraɪd/, *warned* /wɔːnd/, *raised* /reɪzd/

3 If the stem ends in a voiceless consonant (other than /t/), the reduced form is changed to /-t/, e.g.

2.160 *crossed* /krɒst/, *stopped* /stɒpt/, *coughed* /kɒft/

Now try and transcribe these words

2.161 liked, likened, lighted, lied, wiped, washed, rubbed, treated, glued

_____

Notice the past tense of words like *care*:

2.162 cared /kɛəd/

In non-rhotic accents, there is no \<r\> in the transcription. Try

2.163 flared, snared, poured, cured, stirred

_____

Finally, notice an older \<-ed\> form like *learned* used now only as an adjective

2.164 /'lɜːnəd, 'lɜːnɪd/

And these words; transcribe them in the two ways

2.165 blessed _____ _____
      beloved _____ _____

The regular present tense third person inflection \<-es\> also has three possible pronunciations, again depending on the final sound of the stem. The regular plural inflection and the genitive possessive inflection of nouns follow exactly the same pattern.

(1) If the stem ends in /s, z, ʃ, ʒ, tʃ, dʒ/ (the so-called *sibilant* consonants) the inflection is pronounced 'in full', either as /-əz/ or /-ɪz/, e.g.

2.166 *crosses* /'krɒsəz, 'krɒsɪz/

2.167 *watches* /'wɒtʃəz, 'wɒtʃɪz/

2.168 *George's* /'dʒɔːdʒəz, 'dʒɔːdʒɪz/

(Can you detect which one *you* use? It will probably match your choice with \<-ed\>. Are *taxes* and *taxis* the same for you; or possibly *offices* and *officers*?)

(2) If the stem ends in a vowel or a voiced consonant (other than the sibilants), the inflection is pronounced in a reduced form /-z/, e.g.

2.169 *frees* /friːz/, *cries* /kraɪz/, *warns* /wɔːnz/, *John's* /dʒɒnz/

(3) If the stem ends in a voiceless consonant (other than the sibilants), the reduced form is changed to /-s/, e.g.

2.170 *stops* /stɒps/, *coughs* /kɒfs/, *waits/weights* /weɪts/, *Mike's* /maɪks/

There are two cases where an irregular inflection is not reflected in the spelling. Note that the final /s/ of *house* changes to /z/ when the plural suffix is added.

Transcribe

2.171 houses _____

Secondly, a number of words ending in *-th* usually change from the voiceless dental fricative /θ/ to the voiced one /ð/ when the plural suffix is added. Transcribe

2.172 paths, baths, youths, truths, mouths, wreaths

How about these **place names (2)**

2.173	Birmingham	_____	2.181	Nottingham	_____
2.174	Bolton	_____	2.182	Rotherham	_____
2.175	Bristol	_____	2.183	Sheffield	_____
2.176	Ipswich	_____	2.184	Southampton	_____
2.177	Jersey	_____	2.185	Stonehenge	_____
2.178	Manchester	_____	2.186	Washington	_____
2.179	Newcastle	_____	2.187	New York	_____
2.180	Norwich	_____			*(See Key)*

Well done! You have now covered all the vowels and consonants of English!

3 Word Stress

The pronunciation of a word consists of at least one syllable; if a word in English consists of more than one syllable, one syllable will sound more prominent than any other. That greater prominence is what is called **stress**, and we have already introduced the IPA symbol for it [']. The earliest examples we introduced included *snippet*

3.1 /ˈsnɪpɪt/

with the stress on the first syllable, and *exist*

3.2 /ɛgˈzɪst, ɪgˈzɪst/

with the stress on the second syllable.

Stressed syllables contain any of the strong vowels; unstressed syllables contain a weak vowel, and also /ɪ/ or /ʊ/ if at most one consonant follows as in *deceive* and *educate*

3.3 /dɪˈsiːv/, /ˈɛdjʊkeɪt/

However, there is an intermediate degree of stress that occurs in many English words. Take the word *pronunciation* itself; it has five syllables:

3.4 /prə.nʌn.si.eɪ.ʃən/

The fourth syllable /.eɪ./ has the greatest degree of prominence and so will be marked as stressed: /prənʌnsiˈeɪʃən/. The first, third and fifth syllables all contain weak vowels, but the remaining one, the second, has the strong vowel /ʌ/, and sounds too strong to be unstressed, but not strong enough to be the stressed syllable. Hence we make a distinction between the **primary stress** /.eɪ./ and a **secondary stress** /.nʌn./, which is nevertheless heard to be more prominent than **non-stress**, i.e. unstressed syllables. The IPA symbol for secondary stress is a stress mark at the foot of the following syllable: /prəˌnʌnsiˈeɪʃən/.

The identification of secondary stress is important in three types of word: long words which have any number of syllables before the primary stress, a number of homographs, and compound words.

First of all, listen to the four syllables of the word *economic*:

3.5 /iː.kə.nɒm.ɪk/, /ɛ.kə.nɒm.ɪk/

In either pronunciation, which is the syllable with the primary stress? The third one /.ˈnɒm./. The second and fourth syllables both contain weak vowels, but the first contains either the long vowel /iː/ or the short vowel /ɛ/. Both are strong vowels; that first syllable is more prominent than the weak syllables, but not as prominent as the primary stress. Therefore, it has secondary stress: /ˌiːkəˈnɒmɪk/ or /ˌɛkəˈnɒmɪk/.

Now identify the secondary stress in the following words and try to transcribe the whole word

3.6 fundamental, educational, university, scientific, communication

---

These cases of secondary stress are subject to change in phrases like

3.7 *proˈnunciation ˈprinciples, ˈfundamental iˈdeas*

That is one reason why it is important to first identify their secondary stresses as single words. (Briefly, what happens is that the sequence of secondary then primary stress in a word like *pronunciation* /prəˌnʌnsiˈeɪʃən/ is reversed in a phrase like *proˈnunciation ˈprinciples*: /prəˈnʌnsiˌeɪʃən ˈprɪnsɪpəlz/; similarly *ˈfundamental iˈdeas*: /ˈfʌndəˌmentl̩ aɪˈdɪəz/; but all this will be clarified in Chapter 7.)

Secondly, there are a number of homographs in which the ending *-ate* changes pronunciation according to whether they are verbs or not. Take, for instance:

3.8 separate

as an adjective, the *-ate* is pronounced with a neutral vowel: /ˈsɛprət/, but as a verb, the *-ate* is pronounced with a strong vowel: /ˈsɛpəreɪt/. That long vowel is, in fact, another case of secondary stress: /ˈsɛpəˌreɪt/. Now transcribe these homographs in the same two ways

3.9 moderate, advocate, associate, delegate, duplicate, graduate

---

Compound words

Finally, compounds are single words that consist, usually, of two otherwise independent words. To take a simple example, compare the phrase *black bird* with the compound *blackbird* in a statement like:

3.10 *A crow is a black bird, but is bigger than a blackbird.*

The phrase *black bird* has a primary stress on each word: /ˈblæk ˈbɜːd/; but the compound *blackbird* has only one primary stress, on the first part. The second part contains a strong vowel and is treated as a secondary stress: /ˈblækˌbɜːd/.

It is important to note that compounds are sometimes spelt as a single word, or as hyphenated, or with a word space; you could think of three ways of writing this compound

3.11   teatime, tea-time, tea time

However it is spelt, there is only one primary stress. Identify the primary and secondary stresses in the following compounds and transcribe the whole compound word.

Compound check (1)

3.12   teaspoon, coffee cup, dinner plates, lunch box, supper time,

_____

overdone, underneath, hard boiled, half-baked, short-changed

_____   (See Key)

Notice too that a compound itself can become one part of another compound: thus, two secondary stresses are required

3.13   railway, railway lines, railway station _____

It is often the case that the second part of a compound will be reduced to an unstressed syllable with a weak vowel

3.14   Englishman, Scotland, Portsmouth, strawberry, boatswain

_____

Finally, a compound may contain one, or two, bound stems of Greek or Latin origin. The stress pattern depends on the form of the second part; compare *homophone* and *homograph* with primary stress on the first part, and *homorganic* with secondary stress on the first part: /ˈhɒməˌfəʊn/, /ˈhɒməˌɡrɑːf/ and /ˌhɒmɔːˈɡænɪk/.

Compare, and transcribe **Compound check (2)**

3.15
biosphere	_____	biology	_____
equinox	_____	equilibrium	_____
paralanguage	_____	paralinguistic	_____
psychopath	_____	psychology	_____
phoneme	_____	phonological	_____ *(See Key)*

The difference between compounds and phrases will be explored further in Chapter 7.

You have now completed a pretty comprehensive introduction to the transcription of all the words in English not only in the Southern England Standard Pronunciation but also, in a number of cases, in other standards too.

But we haven't finished yet!

We can be a bit more systematic about the differences in accents; we can also be a bit more detailed in variations in individual sounds; we can also take note of what happens when words come together – for instance, the <n>s in *ten green bottles* usually change, in the first case, to /ŋ/, and in the second, to /m/; then we can also take note of the effect of the rhythm of English speech in messages; and finally, we can include intonation which powerfully affects messages.

First of all, we will look at some of the important details of individual sounds – in the way they are made.

4 Allophones

When we introduced the symbol /l/, we noted that linguists usually distinguish between two varieties, known as clear and dark (p. 47). The two varieties never contrast with each other in English and so are never responsible for creating differences in meaning. This is because the two varieties are distributed differently in English words; the distribution of the clear /l/ is confined to a position before vowels (and before /j/), and the distribution of the dark /l/ to a position before consonants (except /j/) and at the end of words. The distribution of the one variety complements the distribution of the other – they can never occur in exactly the same position as the other. That is why they cannot clash, and that is why they are considered as varieties of one phoneme (in English). A phoneme is the basic unit in the phonological system of a language.

Phoneme is a technical word in linguistics and is preferred to the general word *sound*. You might now begin to see why this technical term is necessary. If someone should ask 'How many *l* sounds are there in English?', the answer most (non-linguistics) people would give is "One"; but now *you* know that there are at least these two varieties. The answer thus depends on what perspective a person takes. There is only one *l* sound in the pronunciation (phonological) system, i.e. only one /l/ phoneme; but there are two different sounds from the point of view of actual articulation, i.e. from a purely phonetic perspective. The technical term for varieties of a single phoneme, that show such complementary distribution, is *allophone*. This kind of variation is thus known as allophonic variation.

The form of transcription that we have established so far has focused on phonemes; it has often been referred to as 'broad transcription'. If we wanted to include the details of allophonic variations, we would be turning to 'narrow transcription'. But why would anyone want to do that?

First of all, simply because these variations exist! Because they are there and we can talk about them, we need also a method of referring to them in print. Secondly, if people want to write about phonetic differences in a range of accents of a language, then some kind of 'narrow' transcription is useful. Thirdly, if people want to write about phonetic differences in the pronunciation (phonological systems) of languages, we need a transcription system that captures such details; for example, although both English and French have a phoneme /p/, they are articulated differently, and that phonetic difference can be captured in a 'narrow' transcription. And fourthly, if it is necessary to record differences in individual people's pronunciation, then a 'narrow' transcription is best – for example, for clinical purposes, or for identifying people in a foren-sic context, or comparing children in acquisition studies, or recording students learning a foreign language, etc.

To indicate a 'broad' (phonemic) transcription, the convention is to use slant brackets, / /, as we have done so far. To indicate a 'narrow' (allophonic) transcription, the convention is to use square brackets, [ ]. (In fact, you saw square brackets on page 25 when told how to try and feel the tongue movement in diphthongs; the use of the square brackets was to indicate that the symbols were not to be taken as phonemes.) To illustrate the use of the square brackets, we shall return to the case of the two allophones of the English phoneme /l/. The clear allophone is transcribed as [l], but the dark variety traditionally as [ɫ], or nowadays as [lˠ]. The principle is the same as for phonemes: just as each different phoneme has to be represented by a distinctly different symbol, so each allophone has also to be represented by a distinctly different symbol. The addition of '~'/'ˠ' to the [l] marks the difference between the two forms. Now, you will notice that the same symbol (letter) is used for the phoneme /l/ and the clear allophone [l]; that is precisely why you need to keep the use of the different brackets clear in your mind. Angle brackets, < >, are used to refer to ordinary orthography. Read this sentence as an illustration:

In most English accents, the phoneme /l/, which is usually spelled as <l> or <ll>, is articulated as two distinct allophones: the clear [l] occurs before vowels and the consonant /j/, whereas the dark [ɫ]/[lˠ] occurs before consonants, except /j/, and at the end of words.

Consonants

There are some other important cases of allophonic variation among the con-sonants of English. We will take them in roughly the order in which you learnt to transcribe the consonants.

Aspiration

First of all, the plosives. Three plosives were described (p. 38) as voiceless, /p, t, k/. On most occasions there is a brief delay in the onset of voicing when a vowel or a voiced consonant follows; this brief delay is known as aspira-tion. However, if they are preceded immediately by /s/ at the beginning of a word, this aspiration does not occur. Thus there are two distinct allophones of English /p/: an aspirated variety and an unaspirated variety. (Incidentally, it is the presence of this aspiration that constitutes the main difference between English and French /p/, and /t, k/.) The aspiration is recorded in narrow tran-scription as [ʰ]. Thus aspirated /p/ is transcribed narrowly as [pʰ]; similarly [tʰ] and [kʰ].

Now, the pronunciation of a word like *pin* can be transcribed broadly as /pɪn/, and narrowly as [pʰɪn]. It is exactly the same word, with exactly the same pronunciation, but transcribed in both broad and narrow transcriptions.

Similarly

4.1 tin /___/ and [_____]
kin /___/ and [_____]

What about the *unaspirated* allophone? Simply [pʰ] without the [ʰ]: just [p]! Notice again the importance of the brackets: the same symbol (letter) is used for the phoneme /p/ and the unaspirated allophone [p] – it is the brackets that determines how the symbol is to be interpreted. It is the same with /t/ and [t], and /k/ and [k]. Thus the pronunciation of the word *spin* can be transcribed broadly as /spɪn/ and narrowly as [spɪn]; the latter case shows that the /p/ is the unaspirated allophone. Similarly

4.2 stint /_____/ and [_____]
skin /_____/ and [_____]

This allophonic variation appears in other parts of words too. Take the word

4.3 appear

you can transcribe it both broadly / _____ / and narrowly showing the aspiration of the /p/ [_____]. Now

4.4 aspire

broadly / _____ /, and narrowly, without the aspiration symbol [_____]. Try

4.5 return, disturb

both broadly / _____ /, / _____ /, and narrowly [_____], [_____]. And

4.6 account, askance

broadly / _____ /, /_____ /, and narrowly [_____], [_____]

When /p, t, k/ are followed by silence at the end of an utterance, they are usually aspirated regardless of whether they are preceded by /s/:

4.7 ramp: [ræmpʰ]; grasp: [græspʰ, grɑːspʰ]

Transcribe the following narrowly

4.8 rent: [_____]; rest: [_____]
rink: [_____]; risk: [_____]

Alternatively, they may be simply 'unreleased', i.e. the closure is retained for longer, without the sound of aspiration; in that case the [ʰ] would be inappropriate. If it became necessary to indicate non-release, the symbol [̚] is used. So *help* /hɛlp/ might, in narrow transcription, be either [hɛɫpʰ] or [hɛɫp ̚].
halt /hɒlt/ would either be [_____] or [_____].
think /θɪŋk/ would either be [_____] or [_____].

(The *degree* of aspiration depends on whether /p, t, k/ occur at the beginning of a strong or a weak syllable; if it was ever necessary to distinguish between two degrees of aspiration, then [h] might be used to indicate the stronger form and [ʰ] the weaker: *depend*: [dɪ'pʰɛnd]; *deepen*: ['diːpʰən].)

*

Glottal reinforcement

When /p, t, k/ occur at the end of a syllable before another consonant or before silence, they are typically 'reinforced' by closure at the glottis, as if a glottal stop preceded them. So *map* /mæp/ is pronounced as [mæʔpʰ]; *maps* as [mæʔps]; *map shop* as ['mæʔp͵ʃɒʔpʰ]. Listen:

4.9   map, maps, map shop

Try

4.10   book /bʊk/: [_____]; book shelf: ['___ ͵_____]

4.11   foot /fʊt/: [_____]; footpath: ['___ ͵_____]

You might notice that in the latter case, the [t] might seem to have disappeared completely, as ['fʊʔ͵pɑːθ]; the only trace of /t/ is the [ʔ]. This is now very common all over Britain, and helps to explain how in some accents the /t/ is regularly realized as [ʔ] not only in final position but also in the middle of words, e.g. *what* as [wɒʔ], and *water* as ['wɔːʔə]. Listen

4.12   what, water

*

Voiced flapping

The /t/ is subject to another kind of variation, where between voiced sounds, especially vowels, it acquires voicing and is articulated quickly with a quick 'flap' of the blade of the tongue against the teeth ridge. This is the typical American pronunciation of /t/ in *water*; the symbol for this allophonic variation of /t/ is: [ɾ], e.g. ['wɔːɾə]. This 'flapped' [ɾ] is increasingly heard in SESP and many other accents. Think of the way many people say

4.13   *you'd better, what's the matter with you, but I . . .*

It is typically with [ɾ]: ['bɛɾə], ['maɾə], [bʌɾ aɪ].

Devoicing

The voiced plosives /b, d, g/ lose their voicing 'early' when followed immediately by a voiceless consonant and before silence. A good example is the word *absolutely*; the voicing of /b/ fades in anticipation of the voicelessness of the following /s/; such fading is known as 'devoicing' and can be recorded in a narrow transcription as [̥]: [͵æb̥sə'luːʔli]. *Nab* in a narrow transcription is [næb̥]. (The subscript [̥] is replaced by a superscript [̊] where necessary, e.g. [g̊].) Listen

4.14 absolutely

Now try *lid* in narrow transcription: [___]; and *midst*: [_____]. Listen

4.15 lid, midst

4.16 drug: [___], drug store: ['____ ,____]

Devoicing also affects the voiced fricatives /ʌ, ð, z, ʒ/ and the voiced affricate /dʒ/. *Love* /lʌv/ in narrow transcription is [lʌv̥]; *lovesick* ['lʌv̥ˌsɪʔkʰ]. Listen

4.17 love, lovesick

With in narrow transcription:

4.18 [___]; *with thanks*: [___ '____]

Jazz in narrow transcription:

4.19 [___]; *jazz club*: ['__ ,___]

Rouge in narrow transcription:

4.20 [___]; *rouge stick*: ['__ ,___]

Hedge in narrow transcription:

4.21 [___]; *hedge fund*: ['__ ,___]

Notice too how often such devoicing occurs in verb groups:

4.22 ... *is to* ... [ɪz̥ tu]
... *has to* ... [____ __]
... *have to* ... [____ __]

Another common environment for devoicing is when /l, r, j, w/ follow an aspirated plosive; the aspiration is conveyed by the delay on the onset of their voicing, as in

4.23 play /pleɪ/ [pl̥eɪ]
pray /preɪ/ [___] (but see below for more on /r/)
pew /pjuː/ [___]
queue /kjuː/ [___]
quake /kweɪk/ [_____]

A special case happens when /j/ follows /h/ as in *hew/hue/Hugh*; the /j/ typically takes on the voicelessness of the /h/ totally and becomes itself totally devoiced, with the two phonemes merging into one articulation. There is a special phonetic symbol for the totally voiceless /j/: [ç]. *Hew/hue/Hugh* /hjuː/ is transcribed narrowly as [çuː]. In narrow transcription *huge* is [çuːdʒ̊]. Listen

4.24 /hjuː/, [çuː]; /hjuːdʒ/, [çuːdʒ̊]

Try

4.25   human /ˈhjuːmən/ [_____]

humid /hjuːmɪd/ [_____]

A similar case happens in some accents with many words beginning <wh-> with a pronunciation /hw/, e.g. *whales, which* /hweɪlz/, /hwɪtʃ/ (see pp. 43–44). The /w/ takes on the voicelessness of the /h/ totally, and the two phonemes merge in the same way. The special symbol for the totally voiceless /w/: [ʍ]. So the narrow transcription of these two words is: [ʍeɪlz̥], [ʍɪtʃ]. Try

4.26   why /hwaɪ/ [____]
where /hwɛə/ [____]
whine /hwaɪn/ [____]

*

/r/

English /r/ is described as an approximant; the international symbol is actually [ɹ], as was mentioned on p. 47, and this is the symbol to be used in narrow transcription. So *red* /rɛd/ is transcribed narrowly as [ɹɛd]. However, there is allophonic variation in the phoneme /r/. Notice what typically happens to /r/ in the word *thread* /θrɛd/; it might not be an approximant if there is a very brief contact between /θ/and /ɛ/, a sound that is known technically as a 'tap'. The symbol for it is [ɾ]; so *thread* in narrow transcription is [θɾɛd].

Furthermore, /r/ is fricative immediately after /t, d/; the IPA symbol for this [ɹ̝] – the diacritic [̝] indicates that the [ɹ] is raised (high enough for friction to be created). So *dread* /drɛd/ is transcribed narrowly as [dɹ̝ɛd]. Strictly speaking the 'devoiced' /r/ following aspirated plosives is transcribed as [ɹ̝̊], because it is not only fricative but also devoiced; so *tread* /trɛd/ in narrow transcription should be [tɹ̝̊ɛd]. However, [ɹ̥] is usually used, as a simpler version. (The transcription you entered provisionally for *pray* /preɪ/ [pɹeɪ] above becomes [pɹ̥eɪ].)

Now transcribe the following narrowly

4.27   rust /rʌst/ [_____]
thrust /θrʌst/ [_____]
drudge /drʌdʒ/ [_____]
trust /trʌst/ [_____]

*

Fronting, backing and rounding

The exact place of articulation of a consonant can be affected by adjacent vowels or other consonants. For instance, /m/ is bilabial, but an adjustment typically takes place in informal conversation if /f, v/ follow immediately; the /m/ becomes as labiodental as the /f, v/: test it out on *comfort, some verses*. The lower lip 'backs' towards the upper teeth and so in a technical, phonetic, sense, it has become labiodental; there is a special IPA symbol for a labiodental nasal:

[m̩]. So *comfort* /ˈkʌmfət/ in narrow transcription is [kʰʌɱfəʔtʰ,kʰʌɱfəʔ]; *some verses* /səm ˈvɜːsəz/ is [səɱ ˈvɜːsəz̥]. Similarly /n/ before /f, v/ also becomes labiodental; the articulation is 'fronted'; *inform, in verse* /ɪnˈfɔːm/, /ɪn ˈvɜːs/ in narrow transcription are [ɪɱˈfɔːm], [ɪɱ ˈvɜːs]. In these cases, the fronting and backing are transcribed by a special phonetic symbol.

In other cases, the fronting and backing are indicated by diacritics. /n/ in like manner becomes dental before /θ, ð/; fronting (in this case, towards dental articulation) is transcribed by the diacritic [̪]. *Tenth, in there* /tɛnθ/, /ɪn ˈðɛə/ in narrow transcription are [tʰɛn̪θ], [ɪn̪ ˈðɛə]. The consonants /k, g/ are fronted from a true velar position in the direction of the palatal position when followed immediately by front vowels, e.g. *key, geese* /kiː/, /giːs/ are thus transcribed narrowly as [k̟ʰiː], [g̟iːs]. On the other hand, they are backed from a true velar position when followed immediately by back open vowels, e.g. *car, guard* /kɑː/, /gɑːd/; in narrow transcription they become [k̠ʰɑː], [g̠ɑːd̥].

Rounding, or labialization, of consonants occurs immediately before rounded vowels and /w/. The diacritic to show this is [ʷ]. For example, *soon, twin* /ʃuːn/, /twɪn/ are, in narrow transcription, [sʷuːn], [tʷwɪn].

Fronting, backing and rounding are more or less automatic in English, and so it is usually not felt necessary to indicate them. They are included here simply to alert you to their existence in case it should ever be necessary to include them in a narrow transcription.

*

Summary of allophones for each consonant

Plosives

/p/	**voiceless bilabial**
[pʰ]	aspirated (but with weaker aspiration in unstressed syllables)
[p]	unaspirated after /s/ in a syllable-initial cluster
[ʔp]	glottal reinforcement in syllable-final position before a consonant or silence
[p˺]	unreleased in syllable-final position before a consonant; optional before silence

/paɪ/ [pʰaɪ]; /spaɪ/ [spaɪ]; /mæp/ [mæʔpʰ]; /mæps/ [mæʔps]; /mæp ʃɒp/ [mæʔp˺ ʃɒʔpʰ]

/b/	**voiced bilabial**
[b]	voiced initially and between voiced segments
[b̥]	devoiced before a voiceless consonant or silence
[b˺]	unreleased in syllable-final position before a consonant

/baɪ/ [baɪ]; /beɪbi/ [beɪbi]; /næb/ [næb̥]; /æbsənt/ [æb̥˺səntʰ]

/t/	**voiceless alveolar**
[tʰ]	aspirated (but with weaker aspiration in unstressed syllables)

[t]	unaspirated after /s/ in a syllable-initial cluster
[ʔt, ʔ]	glottal reinforcement or glottal replacement in syllable-final position before a consonant or silence
[t̬]	voiced flap as an alternative between vowels
[t˺]	unreleased in syllable-final position before a consonant
[t̪]	dental before dental consonants
[ṯ]	retracted before /r/

/taɪ/ [tʰaɪ]; /staɪ/ [staɪ]; /fʊt/ [fʊʔtʰ]; /fʊtpɑːθ/ [fʊʔpʰɑːθ], [fʊʔt˺pʰɑːθ]; /bɛtə/ [bɛt̬ə]; /eɪtθ/
[eɪʔt̪θ]; /traɪ/ [ṯɹaɪ]

/d/   **voiced alveolar**

[d]	voiced initially and between voiced segments
[d̥]	devoiced before a voiceless consonant or silence
[d˺]	unreleased in syllable-final position before a consonant
[d̪]	dental before dental consonants
[ḏ]	retracted before /r/

/daɪ/ [daɪ]; /mæd/ [mæd̥]; /mɪdnaɪt/ [mɪd˺naɪʔtʰ]; /wɪdθ/ [wɪd̪θ]; /draɪ/
[ḏɹaɪ]

/k/   **voiceless velar**

[kʰ]	aspirated (but with weaker aspiration in unstressed syllables)
[k]	unaspirated after /s/ in a syllable-initial cluster
[ʔk]	glottal reinforcement in syllable-final position before a consonant or silence
[k˺]	unreleased in syllable-final position before a consonant
[k̟]	advanced before front close vowels
[ḵ]	retracted before back open vowels

/kaɪnd/ [kʰaɪnd̥]; /skaɪ/ [skaɪ]; /bæk/ [bæʔkʰ]; /bækbəʊn/ [bæʔk˺bəʊn];
/kiːp/
[k̟ʰiːʔpʰ]; /kɑː/ [ḵʰɑː]

/g/   **voiced velar**

[g]	voiced initially and between voiced segments
[g̥]	devoiced before a voiceless consonant or silence
[g˺]	unreleased in syllable-final position before a consonant
[g̟]	advanced before front close vowels
[g̱]	retracted before back open vowels

/gaɪ/ [gaɪ]; /næg/ [næg̥]; /ræg bæg/ [ræg˺bæg̥]; /giːs/ [g̟iːs]; /gɑːd/ [g̱ɑːd̥]

Nasals

/m/   **voiced bilabial**

[ɱ]	labiodental before /f, v/
[m]	elsewhere

/kʌmfət/ [kʰʌɱfəʔtʰ]

/n/	**voiced alveolar**
[n̪]	dental before dental consonants
[ɱ]	labiodental before /f, v/
[ɲ]	post-alveolar before /r, s, ʒ, tʃ, dʒ, j/
[n]	elsewhere

/tɛnθ/ [tʰɛn̪θ]; /kən'ʌɜːs/ [kʰəɱ'ʌɜːs]; /lʌntʃ/ [lʌɲtʃ]

/ŋ/	**voiced velar**

(limited distribution – before /k, g/ or in syllable-final position only)

Fricatives

/f/	**voiceless labiodental**
/v/	**voiced labiodental**
[v̥]	devoiced before a voiceless consonant or silence
[v]	elsewhere

/hæv tə .../ [hæv̥ tʰə ...]

/θ/	**voiceless dental**
/ð/	**voiced dental**
[ð̥]	devoiced before a voiceless consonant or silence
[ð]	elsewhere

/wɪð θæŋks/ [wɪð̥ θæŋks]

/s/	**voiceless alveolar**
/z/	**voiced alveolar**
[z̥]	devoiced before a voiceless consonant or silence
[z]	elsewhere

/ɪz tə .../ [ɪz̥ tʰə ...]

/ʃ/	**voiceless palato-alveolar/post-alveolar**
/ʒ/	**voiced palato-alveolar/post-alveolar**
[ʒ̥]	devoiced before a voiceless consonant or silence
[ʒ]	elsewhere
/mɪ'rɑːʒ/ [mɪ'ɹɑːʒ̥]	

/h/	**voiceless glottal**
[ɦ]	voiced between voiced segments

/bɪ'haɪnd/ [bɪ'ɦaɪnd]

(limited distribution – syllable-initial position only)

Affricates

/tʃ/	**voiceless palato-alveolar/post-alveolar**

[ʔtʃ]   glottal reinforcement in syllable-final position before a consonant or silence

[tʃ]   elsewhere

/mætʃ/ [mæʔtʃ]

/dʒ/   **voiced palato-alveolar/post-alveolar**

[d̥ʒ̊]   devoiced before a voiceless consonant or silence

[dʒ]   elsewhere

/hɛdʒ/ [hɛd̥ʒ̊]

Approximants

/l/   **voiced alveolar lateral**

[ɫ]   velarized (dark) before a consonant except /j/ or before silence

[l̪]   dental before /θ, ð/

[l̥]   devoiced after aspirated /p, k/

[l]   elsewhere

/bɪl/ [bɪɫ]; /bɪld/ [bɪɫd]; /bɪljən/ [bɪljən]; /wɛlθ/ [wɛl̪θ]; /pleɪ/ [pl̥eɪ]

/r/   **voiced post-alveolar**

[ɾ]   tap after /θ, ð/

[ɹ̝]   fricative after /d/

[ɹ̥]   devoiced after aspirated /p, t, k/

[ɹ]   elsewhere

/θriː/ [θriː]; /draɪ/ [d̥ɹ̝aɪ]; /preɪ/ [pɹ̥eɪ]; /rɛd/ [ɹɛd]
(limited distribution – syllable-initial position only)

/j/   **voiced palatal**

[j̊]   devoiced after aspirated /p, t, k/

[ç]   for /hj.../

[j]   elsewhere

/tjuːn/ [tjuːn]; /hjuːdʒ/ [çuːdʒ]
(limited distribution – syllable-initial position only)

/w/   **voiced labial-velar**

[w̥]   devoiced after aspirated /p, t, k/

([ʍ]   for /hw../)

[w]   elsewhere

/kwiːn/ [kw̥iːn]; (/hwaɪl/ [ʍaɪɫ])
(limited distribution – syllable-initial position only)

Vowels

There are three processes that affect the articulation of all the vowels of English: nasalization, clipping and breaking; and two other processes that affect the articulation of just the long vowels: smoothing and diphthongization.

Nasalization

Vowels adjacent to nasal consonants 'catch' something of their nasal quality. This nasalization of the vowels is more or less automatic and would not necessarily be transcribed. But if needed, the symbol is [˜]. So *man* /mæn/ in narrow transcription is [mæ̃n]; *sunk* /sʌŋk/ is [sʌ̃ŋkʰ]; *neat* /niːt/ is [nĩˑʔtʰ]. Nasalization in English is not phonemic as it is in French for instance; when French loan words are pronounced in English, some speakers choose to include the nasalization as in French, e.g. *liaison* /li'eɪzɒ̃/ instead of the more usual /li'eɪzən/. Listen

4.28 /li'eɪzɒ̃/

*

Clipping

Clipping refers to the shortening of vowels in syllables that are closed with voiceless consonants. The length of a vowel – whether it is a short vowel, a long monophthong or a diphthong, or even a weak vowel – is roughly only half the length that it is in open syllables or syllables closed by voiced consonants. This clipping can, obviously, be recognized more easily in long vowels than in vowels that are by nature already relatively short. Clipping does not alter the quality of the vowel, so no change to the symbol is necessary. If it *is* necessary to mark clipping, this can be done by replacing [ː] with [ˑ] with long vowels, and by adding [˘] over short and diphthongal vowels.

Listen to the difference in the length of the vowel in *sea, seat*. Both are transcribed with the vowel /iː/ in a broad transcription, but it is possible to show the allophonic difference in a narrow transcription: [siː], [siˑʔtʰ]. Also *side, sight* (*site/cite*), and *Sid, sit*: [saɪd̥], [saɪ̆ʔtʰ]; [sɪd̥], [sɪ̆ʔtʰ].

*

Breaking

Breaking refers to the transitional sound between a vowel and a dark /l/ [ɫ]. It was referred to on p. 47 with an explanation that the transitional sound is similar to /ə/. In a narrow transcription, breaking is indicated by that symbol, but raised: [ᵊ] to show that it does not constitute a separate syllable. So the examples given there are transcribed narrowly as

feel /fiːl/ [fiːᵊɫ]
fool /fuːl/ [fuːᵊɫ]
fail /feɪl/ [feɪᵊɫ]
Now transcribe the others:
file/phial /faɪl/ [ ]
foil /fɔɪl/ [ ]

foal /fəʊl/ [   ]
foul/fowl /faʊl/ [   ]

Historically, something similar happened before /r/. Modern SESP has *serious, furious, various* as

4.29   /sɪərɪəs/, /fjʊərɪəs/, /vɛərɪəs/

but other accents still retain a long monophthong before /r/:

4.30   /siːrɪəs/, /fjuːrɪəs/, /vɛːrɪəs/

Again historically, when /r/ was lost in SESP, the 'breaking' to [ə] remained, producing the centring diphthongs: /ɪə, ʊə, ɛə/ (and also /ɔə/ in some accents still).

✳

Smoothing

The tongue movement for long vowels, whether monophthong or diphthong, may be reduced when followed by a weak vowel. For example, the word *hour* has a closing diphthong /aʊ/ before the weak vowel /ə/; some speakers choose to reduce the amount of tongue movement by 'smoothing' out the closing movement of the diphthong, reducing the articulation to [aə]. (Many speakers reduce the tongue movement even further with the possessive determiner *our* /ɑː/!). *liable* /ˈlaɪəbəl/ becomes [ˈlaəbəɫ]. Listen:

4.31   liable

Thus some speakers make no distinction between *tower* /taʊə/ and *tire* /taɪə/: [tʰaə]; others do maintain a difference with distinct starting positions:

4.32   [tʰɑə], [tʰaə].

ruin likewise may be either /ruːɪn/ or /rʊɪn/; listen for the difference:

4.33   ruin

The latter shows how the tongue movement from a long monophthong to a weak vowel can be 'smoothed'. *foreseeable* may be either /fɔːˈsiːəbəl/ or /fɔːˈsɪəbəl/:

4.34   foreseeable

✳

Diphthongization

The two close long monophthongs /iː, uː/ are liable to diphthongization. Instead of a steady tongue position, there is a tendency to start from a relatively open position and move to the close position: [ɪi, ʊu]. Listen to a fairly common pronunciation of the words *tea, too*:

4.35 [tʰɪi], [tʰʊu]

The descriptions of smoothing and diphthongization touch upon alternative pronunciations that speakers may adopt, and so we begin to enter the area of accents, which is the next big topic that we need to deal with.

5 Accents

Everybody speaks differently – even identical twins! People with the same English accent have the same phonological system and a high degree of consistency in articulation, but their voices are still distinctly different. It might be possible to transcribe all these individual differences – voice quality, pitch level, tone, speed, etc., but our interest is the transcription of more general properties of pronunciation.

An accent indicates a person's identification with a community of people. English accents vary according to geography – national and regional types, e.g. British, American, Indian, Scottish, English Midlands, North Walian English, Ulster and so on. We could add here foreign accents too; non-native speakers of English share particular features with others from the same linguistic background. Accents also vary in a historical perspective; the pronunciation of the younger generation of today sounds quite different in some respects from that of their grandparents, for instance. This is how historical change comes about over the centuries, with slight changes of pronunciation in successive generations. Accents also vary socially; typically, dockers and doctors from the same city are expected to sound very different. There are also gender differences; think of the way many young women say 'Thank you', with a vowel that seems half way to saying 'Thank ye'; most British men do not pronounce that phrase with that kind of vowel change. Finally, there are stylistic variations, where pronunciation changes according to the formality of the setting; 'Do you want a cup of tea?' can sound more like 'Joanna Cupper' in an informal setting!

Whatever type of accent – geographical, foreign, historical, social or stylistic – differences between them can be categorized in four ways. One accent may differ from another in their **phonological inventories**. For instance, SESP has the vowel phoneme /ʌ/ in a word like *strut*, but many people with a Northern English accent use the vowel /ʊ/ instead and simply never the use the /ʌ/ vowel; there is no /ʌ/ in their system at all. Look back at p. 16. They have therefore a different phonological system. It is also well known that the so-called General American accent does not include the vowel phoneme /ɒ/ – another instance of a phonological inventory difference.

One accent may also differ from another in **phonetic features**. Younger speakers of SESP pronounce *trap* with an opener vowel [a] than older speakers of SESP [æ] – think of the Queen! Look back at p. 13. This is a phonetic variation of the *same* phoneme, so this is not a difference in inventories. Also, many working-class Londoners regularly pronounce /t/ as [ʔ] in the middle and at the end of words as in *hot water* (see p. 63). The [ʔ] is a *phonetic* variation in this context to [tʰ]; it is not an extra phoneme in the inventory. That final vowel in

5.1 *thank you*

as pronounced by many young women is a more central close vowel: [ʉ] or [ʊː]; again, this is not an extra phoneme, but a phonetic variation of /uː/ in the context of the /j/ consonant.

An accent may also differ in the way a phoneme may be distributed, i.e. in the places in a word where it can occur. This distributional variation may be phonological or lexical. A well-known example of **phonological distribution** differences is the distinction between rhotic and non-rhotic accents. Southern England Standard Pronunciation, as we have seen, is non-rhotic in that the phoneme /r/ cannot occur before a consonant or before silence. The General American (GA) accent, which is rhotic, has the same phoneme /r/ but it does allow it to occur before a consonant and before silence; the difference is simply distributional. *Farm* in GA is /fɑrm/; in SESP it is /fɑːm/. There is no difference in the inventories of phonemes in the two accents, nor necessarily a difference in phonetic form; merely a difference in the distribution of that particular phoneme. Another example was touched on on p. 71: the vowel phoneme /iː/ can appear before /r/ in some accents as in *serious*, but in SESP it cannot; the vowel before /r/ must be /ɪə/ in SESP. This again is a distributional difference; the phoneme inventory is no different, nor the phonetic realization of either vowel.

Lexical distribution refers to instances where a phoneme can appear in the same phonological context as a rule, but not in a particular word or group of words. Southern England Standard Pronunciation and most other accents in Britain allow both /θ, ð/ in word-final position, but whereas most accents in England and Wales have /ð/ at the end of *with*, most Scottish accents have /θ/. In this case, the 'choice' of phoneme depends on the particular word. Another well-known lexical distribution difference distinguishes SESP from many other accents in Britain; there is a group of words that take /ɑː/ typically in words that have a voiceless consonant following, e.g. *class*, whereas other accents take /æ/. But we cannot establish a rule for all such cases because even SESP has /mæs/ for *mass*; and *nasty* /ˈnɑːsti/ and *pasty* /ˈpæsti/ do not rhyme in SESP. Look back at p. 20. So there is no general rule that establishes a difference in the *phonological* distribution of the two vowels; rather, it depends on the selection of the word(s) – it is a case of a different *lexical* distribution.

These four kinds of difference affect both consonants and vowels, and also word stress. There are a number of instances of word stress differences between British and American accents. Consider these few words:

5.2 frustrate, cremate, vacate

In two-syllable verbs of this kind ending in /-eɪt/, British speakers place the primary stress on that final syllable: /ˌfrʌˈstreɪt/; /krəˈmeɪt/; /vəˈkeɪt/; whereas American speakers tend to place the primary stress on the first syllable:

5.3 /ˈfrʌˌstreɪt/; /ˈkriːˌmeɪt/; /ˈveɪˌkeɪt/

This is a case of phonological distribution. So is the difference between British *secondary* /ˈsɛkəndri/ and American /ˈsɛkənˌdɛri/; and all those words that have final <-ary>, <-ery>, <-ory> and <-ury> without primary stress. A lexical difference is found in the noun *address*: British /əˈdrɛs/ and American /ˈædrɛs/. Compare also

aristocrat: British /ˈærɪstəˌkræt/; American /əˈrɪstəˌkræt/

harass: British /ˈhærəs/; American /həˈræs/

magazine : British /ˌmægəˈziːn/; American /ˈmægəziːn/.

5.4 *address, aristocrat, harass, magazine*

Lexical sets

To illustrate all these variations and give you some practice in observing them and transcribing them, ten English speakers were recorded reading a set of words in their different accents, and then an eleventh person who speaks English as a foreign language was added. Their accents differ in geography, social class, generation, gender and in linguistic background. Their voices are not meant to necessarily represent a stereotypical accent, so not every well-known feature of a particular accent may be present in their pronunciation. The recordings were made in natural settings, not in a studio; the spoken data that you may have to transcribe one day will almost certainly be recorded in natural settings, and you will have to contend with a certain amount of background noise, like the hum of a kitchen fridge, a mobile phone ringing, a door opening, etc.

The eleven accents are, first, from the USA, then four regions of England (London, the West Country, the Midlands and the North) and three other countries within the UK – Scotland, Wales and Northern Ireland – followed by two speakers of English as a second language, from Africa and India, and finally, a Chinese visitor to UK, representing a foreign accent.

They all use the same words, more or less, so that you can compare their pronunciation, particularly of the vowels, in a methodical way. These **lexical sets** have been chosen to represent typical variations in the way vowels are pronounced across a wide spectrum of English accents. The idea of lexical sets derives from the work of John Wells (see especially Wells 1982); each word contains one particular vowel, which varies across a number of accents. The lexical set in this workbook follows in the main the words chosen in Chapter 1. The thirty words represent different aspects of vowel articulation and so it is necessary to listen carefully for any variations from the qualities that have been practised and transcribed so far. The thirty words are:

5.5 1. **lick**
2. **leg**
3. **lack**
4. **lock**

5. **look**
6. **luck**
7. **leak**
8. **lark**
9. **palm**
10. **pork**
11. **Paul**
12. **Luke**
13. **blew**
14. **lurk**
15. **earth**
16. **waist**
17. **lake**
18. **like**
19. **void**
20. **know**
21. **load**
22. **loud**
23. **pier**
24. **pair**
25. **poor**
26. **coffee**
27. **Fiona**
28. **Louise**
29. **farmer**
30. **drama**

The first six words contain the short vowels. Listen for vowel quality: note that some accents do not distinguish all six (i.e. differences in phonological inventories). Listen also for vowel quantity; are some vowels sometimes pronounced long?

The next words from 7 to 25 contain the long vowels: monophthongs and diphthongs (front closing, back closing and centring). Listen particularly to variations in quality: some diphthongs are pronounced as monophthongs, and some monophthongs as diphthongs with a bit of a glide. Some accents distinguish *blew* from *blue*; listen for distinctions in other such pairs of words too (i.e., again, differences in phonological inventories). Listen also for variations in quantity, especially as some pronunciations are rhotic (i.e. differences in phonological distribution). You might notice variations in the pronunciation of /r/ as well (i.e. phonetic realization). What about the /l/ in *Paul*? Is it pronounced, and if so, how? Listen out for other phonetic variations of consonants, especially among the non-native speakers of English.

The final five contain the weak vowels: /i/ in final position and before another vowel; /u/, and final /ə/. Do the very last two words rhyme in your accent? Do they rhyme for all of the speakers?

These are the main things to listen for. Try and transcribe each word in full, or at least identify the phonetic quality of the vowels using a narrow transcription where necessary. You will find a key and some general remarks in the appendix, but DO NOT look at them *before* you have listened to some of the voices and attempted a transcription. Try and transcribe a few of them, if not all of them!

USA

Tim is a language teacher, in his 30s, from Ohio. He does not have a broad American accent, but it is rhotic. Notice what tends to happen to his vowels before /r/ compared to SESP. Listen carefully to the vowel qualities in 23–25.

5.6
1. lick   _____
2. leg   _____
3. lack   _____
4. lock   _____
5. look   _____
6. luck   _____
7. leak   _____
8. lark   _____
9. palm   _____
10. pork   _____
11. Paul   _____
12. Luke   _____
13. blew   _____
14. lurk   _____
15. earth   _____
16. waist   _____
17. lake   _____
18. like   _____
19. void   _____
20. know   _____
21. load   _____
22. loud   _____
23. pier   _____
24. pair   _____
25. poor   _____
26. coffee _____
27. Fiona   _____
28. Louise _____
29. farmer _____
30. drama   _____

London

Maureen is a retired social worker, in her 60s, from Balham. She does not have a real Cockney accent, but listen to see if 11 and 25 are different or not. Listen to what happens to SESP centring diphthongs (23–25). How does her pronunciation of *Louise* differ from SESP?

5.7
1. lick _____
2. leg _____
3. lack _____
4. lock _____
5. look _____
6. luck _____
7. leak _____
8. lark _____
9. palm _____
10. pork _____
11. Paul _____
12. Luke _____
13. blew _____
14. lurk _____
15. earth _____
16. waist _____
17. lake _____
18. like _____
19. void _____
20. know _____
21. load _____
22. loud _____
23. pier _____
24. pair _____
25. poor _____
26. coffee _____
27. Fiona _____
28. Louise _____
29. farmer _____
30. drama _____

West Country

Lisa is a housewife and gardener, in her 40s, from Fishponds, Bristol. Listen to whether her accent is rhotic or not. A well-known feature of the Bristolian accent is the tendency to add /l/ to words ending in a vowel; for that reason, item 23 was changed to *idea*, to see whether she does. Does she? Does she add it to *drama*? What happens to the final /l/ in *Paul*? How are *Paul* and *poor* distinguished, compared to the Londoner's voice?

5.8   1.   **lick**   _____
      2.   **leg**   _____
      3.   **lack**   _____
      4.   **lock**   _____
      5.   **look**   _____
      6.   **luck**   _____
      7.   **leak**   _____
      8.   **lark**   _____
      9.   **palm**   _____
     10.   **pork**   _____
     11.   **Paul**   _____
     12.   **Luke**   _____
     13.   **blew**   _____
     14.   **lurk**   _____
     15.   **earth**   _____
     16.   **waist**   _____
     17.   **lake**   _____
     18.   **like**   _____
     19.   **void**   _____
     20.   **know**   _____
     21.   **load**   _____
     22.   **loud**   _____
     23.   **idea**   _____
     24.   **pair**   _____
     25.   **poor**   _____
     26.   **coffee** _____
     27.   **Fiona**   _____
     28.   **Louise** _____
     29.   **farmer** _____
     30.   **drama**   _____

Midlands

Chris is a salesman in an electrical goods store, in his 30s, from Birmingham. How does he distinguish between *look* and *luck*? Does he pronounce *Paul* with /l/? Listen to the vowel qualities of the closing diphthongs; notice how they start and how they finish. How do his pronunciations of 23–25 compare with SESP?

5.9   1.   **lick**   _____
      2.   **leg**   _____
      3.   **lack**   _____
      4.   **lock**   _____
      5.   **look**   _____
      6.   **luck**   _____
      7.   **leak**   _____

8. lark   _____
9. palm   _____
10. pork   _____
11. Paul   _____
12. Luke   _____
13. blew   _____
14. lurk   _____
15. earth   _____
16. waist   _____
17. lake   _____
18. like   _____
19. void   _____
20. know   _____
21. load   _____
22. loud   _____
23. pier   _____
24. pair   _____
25. poor   _____
26. coffee   _____
27. Fiona   _____
28. Louise   _____
29. farmer   _____
30. drama   _____

North of England

Another Tim; a student, in his 20s, from Easingwold, Yorkshire. He hesitates before item 6; can you guess why? Listen to the vowels of items 8 and 9, and then to the vowels of 10, 11 and 25, and compare them all with SESP. How do his pronunciations of 23–25 compare with SESP?

5.10
1. lick   _____
2. leg   _____
3. lack   _____
4. lock   _____
5. look   _____
6. luck   _____
7. leak   _____
8. lark   _____
9. palm   _____
10. pork   _____
11. Paul   _____
12. Luke   _____
13. blew   _____
14. lurk   _____
15. earth   _____

16.	waist	_____
17.	lake	_____
18.	like	_____
19.	void	_____
20.	know	_____
21.	load	_____
22.	loud	_____
23.	idea	_____
24.	pair	_____
25.	poor	_____
26.	coffee	_____
27.	Fiona	_____
28.	Louise	_____
29.	farmer	_____
30.	drama	_____

Scotland

Shona is a teacher, in her 40s, from Bearsden, Glasgow. She does not have a broad Scottish accent, but notice how her articulation of /uː/ and /ʊ/ are fronted, compared to SESP. Is her accent rhotic? What difference does this make to vowel quantity? And to vowel quality in some cases? Notice too how diphthongs in SESP are monophthongs in her accent. Do the final items rhyme? What quality do you detect in final unstressed <a> in *Fiona* and *drama*? Is it different from SESP /ə/?

5.11	1.	lick	_____
	2.	leg	_____
	3.	lack	_____
	4.	lock	_____
	5.	look	_____
	6.	luck	_____
	7.	leak	_____
	8.	lark	_____
	9.	palm	_____
	10.	pork	_____
	11.	Paul	_____
	12.	Luke	_____
	13.	blew	_____
	14.	lurk	_____
	15.	earth	_____
	16.	waist	_____
	17.	lake	_____
	18.	like	_____
	19.	void	_____
	20.	know	_____

21.	**load**	_____
22.	**loud**	_____
23.	**idea**	_____
24.	**pair**	_____
25.	**poor**	_____
26.	**coffee**	_____
27.	**Fiona**	_____
28.	**Louise**	_____
29.	**farmer**	_____
30.	**drama**	_____

Wales

Gordon is a retired sub-postmaster, in his 60s, from Aberdare, South Wales. He is bilingual. Welsh is 'rhotic' phonologically; listen to see whether his English therefore is also rhotic. For him, *blew* is pronounced differently from *blue*; so *blue* replaces *Luke* as item 12, so that you can observe the difference. *Know* and *no* are also different for him; so *no* replaces *load*, so that you can observe that difference too. Similarly, *waste* is different from *waist*; however, there is only the merest hint of the difference in this recording; *waste* replaces *lake*. Also, listen carefully to his rendering of the SESP centring diphthongs; which words seem to be pronounced as two syllables?

5.12	1.	**lick**	_____
	2.	**leg**	_____
	3.	**lack**	_____
	4.	**lock**	_____
	5.	**look**	_____
	6.	**luck**	_____
	7.	**leak**	_____
	8.	**lark**	_____
	9.	**palm**	_____
	10.	**pork**	_____
	11.	**Paul**	_____
	12.	**blue**	_____
	13.	**blew**	_____
	14.	**lurk**	_____
	15.	**earth**	_____
	16.	**waist**	_____
	17.	**waste**	_____
	18.	**like**	_____
	19.	**void**	_____
	20.	**know**	_____
	21.	**no**	_____
	22.	**loud**	_____
	23.	**idea**	_____

24.	pair	_____
25.	poor	_____
26.	coffee	_____
27.	Fiona	_____
28.	Louise	_____
29.	farmer	_____
30.	drama	_____

Northern Ireland

Jennifer is a trainee food technologist, in her 20s, from Armagh. Her pronunciation is in some ways the most difficult to transcribe! Can you hear a difference from SESP in vowel quality in the very first word, and a difference in vowel quantity in the second? What vowel quality do you hear in item 6? Is her accent rhotic? Check for /r/ before consonants (items 8, 10, 14), and then in final position (23–25, 29). For her, the vowels in *Luke* and *blew* are different, but not in quite the same way as for the Welsh speaker. Listen for differences in *waist* and *lake* too. You might then expect the vowels in *know* and *load* also to be different; but are they? How many syllables do you hear in items 23–25? Finally, in what ways do the final two words differ?

5.13			
	1.	lick	_____
	2.	leg	_____
	3.	lack	_____
	4.	lock	_____
	5.	look	_____
	6.	luck	_____
	7.	leak	_____
	8.	lark	_____
	9.	palm	_____
	10.	pork	_____
	11.	Paul	_____
	12.	Luke	_____
	13.	blew	_____
	14.	lurk	_____
	15.	earth	_____
	16.	waist	_____
	17.	lake	_____
	18.	like	_____
	19.	void	_____
	20.	know	_____
	21.	load	_____
	22.	loud	_____
	23.	idea	_____
	24.	pair	_____
	25.	poor	_____

26. coffee   _____
27. Fiona   _____
28. Louise   _____
29. farmer   _____
30. drama   _____

Africa

Judy is an administrator in UK higher education, in her 40s, from the Luhya speaking region of Kenya; she also speaks Swahili. Luhya and Swahili have much simpler vowel systems than English; what evidence of that fact appears in her pronunciation of English? One clue is that the distinction between short and long vowels is hardly noticeable in her pronunciation of English. Listen also for any difference there might be between the vowels of *Luke* and *blew*; *waist* and *lake*; and *know* and *no*.

5.14
1. lick   _____
2. leg   _____
3. lack   _____
4. lock   _____
5. look   _____
6. luck   _____
7. leak   _____
8. lark   _____
9. palm   _____
10. pork   _____
11. Paul   _____
12. Luke   _____
13. blew   _____
14. lurk   _____
15. earth   _____
16. waist   _____
17. lake   _____
18. like   _____
19. void   _____
20. know   _____
21. no   _____
22. loud   _____
23. idea   _____
24. pair   _____
25. poor   _____
26. coffee _____
27. Fiona   _____
28. Louise _____
29. farmer _____
30. drama   _____

India

Bhaskarrao is a postman, in his 60s, from Visakhapatnam, Andhra Pradesh. He has been in UK for about 15 years. His first language is Telegu; he also speaks Hindi and Urdu, which all have simpler vowel systems than English, and evidence of that will appear in his pronunciation. You might notice that initial plosives are not aspirated, whereas final plosives are; check on how to transcribe the difference in narrow transcription. Is his accent rhotic? In some cases it is difficult to tell, but in items 23–25, it is quite clear; but is the /r/ a tap [ɾ] or an approximant [ɹ]? His pronunciation of *pier* follows spelling and maybe idiosyncratic; he confirmed he knew what the word referred to. Finally, note how the final two words differ.

5.15
1. lick   _____
2. leg   _____
3. lack   _____
4. lock   _____
5. look   _____
6. luck   _____
7. leak   _____
8. lark   _____
9. palm   _____
10. pork   _____
11. Paul   _____
12. Luke   _____
13. blew   _____
14. lurk   _____
15. earth   _____
16. waist   _____
17. lake   _____
18. like   _____
19. void   _____
20. know   _____
21. load   _____
22. loud   _____
23. idea   _____
24. pair   _____
25. poor   _____
26. coffee   _____
27. Fiona   _____
28. Louise   _____
29. farmer   _____
30. drama   _____

A foreign accent

Wayne is from China, an economics teacher, in his 30s, from Dalian; he speaks Mandarin as his mother tongue. He was recorded two weeks after arriving in UK, on his first ever visit to an English-speaking country. Mandarin has a simpler vowel system than English; notice, for instance the vowel qualities in the very first two words. Notice how varied the vowel length is in his pronunciation of SESP long vowels. The open transition between /b/ and /l/ in *blew* is transcribed with a raised [ᵊ]. His pronunciation of *pair* may be idiosyncratic. Where is the word stress in his pronunciation of *Louise*? Finally, the final two words do not quite rhyme; but how do they differ?

5.16

1. lick   _____
2. leg   _____
3. lack   _____
4. lock   _____
5. look   _____
6. luck   _____
7. leak   _____
8. lark   _____
9. palm   _____
10. pork   _____
11. Paul   _____
12. Luke   _____
13. blew   _____
14. lurk   _____
15. earth   _____
16. waist   _____
17. lake   _____
18. like   _____
19. void   _____
20. know   _____
21. load   _____
22. loud   _____
23. idea   _____
24. pair   _____
25. poor   _____
26. coffee   _____
27. Fiona   _____
28. Louise   _____
29. farmer   _____
30. drama   _____

Remember you can check your transcriptions against the Key in the appendix and read some general comments there about consistencies and trends.

Chapters 4 and 5 contain a lot of technical detail and are pitched at a more advanced academic level than the preceding three chapters. We now return to a more gentle style for novices in transcription as we move on beyond individual words to combinations of words in phrases, focusing mainly on a broad transcription again.

6 Phrases

Words do not usually come by themselves, but are accompanied by many others! As words come together, they affect each other, usually to make the transition between one word and the next smoother.

Take a simple example like *Ten green bottles*. Most people would recognize this phrase as the title of an old song and would probably say it quickly and without any hesitation. As they did so, they probably would not notice that the pronunciation of *ten* and *green* changes because of the contact each has with adjacent words. In this case, *ten* would probably be pronounced with its /n/ changing to /ŋ/ in anticipation of its contact with the /g/ of *green*; and *green* would probably be pronounced with its /n/ changing to /m/ in anticipation of its contact with the /b/ of *bottles*. These kinds of change reflect a process known as simplification, which is the equivalent in pronunciation to processes like economy of effort, or 'cutting corners', in other spheres of life. In these cases, the two /n/s have changed to suit their contexts by becoming a little bit more similar to the consonants that follow in the next word.

Other ways of 'cutting corners' in pronunciation include leaving sounds out or putting extra 'transitional' sounds in to facilitate smooth contacts. These simplification processes are typical of most informal conversational speech, which is what we engage in most of the time when we are talking. They can, however, be countered if the need is felt for a precise articulation in informal conversation and, in any case, in more formal speech. We will be assuming an informal conversational style of speech for the most part in this Chapter.

＊

Assimilation

The adjustment of the articulation of words as a consequence of their immediate spoken environment can happen in various ways. When an adjustment is made to accommodate an actual phonetic feature in the immediate environment, that process of simplification is known as assimilation. The adjustment makes the phoneme more similar to its environment. The adjustment of the /n/ in *ten* to the velar articulation of the /g/ in *green* is a case of assimilation: the /n/ becomes velar /ŋ/ which shares an identical feature with the velar articulation of /g/. Similarly, the /n/ of *green* becomes bilabial /m/ in anticipation of the bilabial articulation of /b/ in *bottles*.

Word-final /n/ regularly adjusts itself in English to the anticipated point of articulation of the consonant at the beginning of the next word. Think of common phrases with the prepositions *on* and *in* which are followed by words beginning with bilabial /p, b, m/ and you will notice that the /n/ easily adjusts itself to /m/ in anticipation.

6.1   on purpose   /ɒm ˈpɜːpəs/   in person   /ɪm ˈpɜːsn̩/

Now listen to and transcribe

6.2   on paper   _____   in print   _____
      on principle   _____   in prison   _____

      on behalf   _____   in between   _____
      on balance   _____   in Bristol   _____

      on Monday   _____   in March   _____
      on my behalf   _____   in medicine   _____

Notice that in cases like *on Monday* and *in March*, there is a 'double' /mm/, a single articulation of double length to account for the final /m/ of *on* and *in* and the initial /m/ of the following word. Otherwise it would sound like

6.3   om unday   im arch

which does not sound typical of native English speech.

In a parallel way, word-final /n/ easily adjusts to a velar /ŋ/ in anticipation of following velar consonants /k, g/.

6.4   on call   /ɒŋ ˈkɔːl/   in case   /ɪŋ ˈkeɪs/

Listen and transcribe

6.5   on course   _____   in keeping   _____
      on guard   _____   in Gloucester _____
      on grass   _____   in goal   _____

An identical case of assimilation occurs in the prefixes *un-* and *in-* (whether it means 'in' or negative). Listen and transcribe

6.6   unpleasant   /ʌmˈplɛznt/   input   /ˈɪmpʊt/
      unbalanced   _____   inbuilt   _____
      unmade   _____   inmate   _____
      unkind   _____   incorrect   _____
      ungrateful   _____   ingratitude   _____

Now consider these phrases and note the assimilation process:

6.7   10p   /ˈtɛm ˈpiː/   10 quid   /ˈtɛŋ ˈkwɪd/
      £1   _____   one go   _____
      fine mess   _____   fine grain   _____
      gun boat   _____   gun carrier   _____

| hen party | _____ | hen coop | _____ |
| ten pin bowling | _____ | 7 cases | _____ |

All these cases of /n/ assimilation involve adjustments from one phoneme, /n/, to another, /m, ŋ/. These are instances of *phonemic* assimilation. But the same kind of assimilation occurs in

6.8

in fun	ten things	sunrise	in waves
in fact	one thought	on show	on Wednesday
on vacation	in there	John Jones	runway
in verse	in theory	in use	ten weeks

But the resulting articulation from the assimilation process is not identical to an existing phoneme: there is the labiodental nasal [ɱ] before the labiodental /f, v/, the dental nasal [n̪] before the dental /θ, ð/, and either a post-alveolar or palatal nasal [ɲ] before /r, ʃ, tʃ, dʒ, j/. Look back at pp. 65–66. These are instances of *allophonic* assimilation, since the adjustments do not coincide with other identifiable phonemes, and so are not recorded in a *phonemic* transcription.

Assimilation of final /n/ is common in many other languages, including Latin, where the bilabial assimilation was actually expressed in the orthography: *in + possibilis > impossibilis*. As a result we have spellings like *impossible, improper, impress, imbalance, imbecile, immense, immeasurable* in English. And *impromptu* from Italian.

*

Assimilation of **final /d/** in English is almost parallel to that of /n/, but this is not matched in many other languages. The /d/ becomes bilabial /b/ – retaining its voicing – before bilabial /p, b, m/, and becomes velar /g/ before velar /k, g/. (This is true of most English accents, though West Walian English is an exception.) Notice the process in

6.9

bad penny	/ˈbæb ˈpɛni/	red kite	/ˈrɛg ˈkaɪt/
good boy	_____	bad girl	_____
red meat	_____	good gracious	_____

Notice it too in the greetings:

6.10 good morning   /ˈgʊb ˈmɔːnɪŋ/ goodbye /ˈgʊb ˈbaɪ/

Notice that in cases like *good boy, goodbye*, there is a 'double' /bb/ – a single articulation of double length to account for the final /b/ in /gʊb/ and the initial /b/ of the following word; likewise, a 'double' /gg/ in *bad girl*.

But final /d/ may also for some speakers become post-alveolar /dʒ/ before palatal /j/. Notice the process in

6.11 a bad year /ə ˈbædʒ ˈjɜː/   good use   /ˈgʊdʒ ˈjuːs/

Note the subtle difference in articulation between *good use* and

6.12 *good juice* /ˈɡʊd ˈdʒuːs/

Historically, this post-alveolar assimilation of /d/ before /j/ accounts for the /dʒ/ in words like

6.13 *grandeur, verdure, soldier*

and, more recently, in

educate, gradual

(Standard South Walian English keeps the /dj/ sequence in *soldier*: /ˈsəʊldjə/.) Many transfer this process also to the beginnings of words as in

6.14 *due, duty* /ˈdʒuː/, /ˈdʒuːti/

Note that this historical instance of assimilation does not apply in US English. The same kind of allophonic assimilation occurs in phrases like

6.15 good fun   a bad thing   a red shirt

which we noted with /n/ above.

⋆

Assimilation of **final /t/** in English used to be exactly parallel to assimilation of final /d/, producing /p/ and /k/ – retaining voicelessness – before bilabial /b, d, m/ and velar /k, ɡ/. Thus *hot potato* would be /ˈhɒp pəˈteɪtəʊ/ and *white cross* /ˈwaɪk ˈkrɒs/. But a new tendency has developed and that is to articulate final /t/ as a glottal stop [ʔ]. Look back at p. 63. This produces *hot* as [ˈhɒʔ] and *white* as [ˈwaɪʔ], which eliminates any possibility of assimilation. Listen to the two possibilities in the following phrases:

6.16 hot [ʔ] potato   hot /p/ potato   white [ʔ] cross   white /k/ cross
      not [ʔ] bad   not /p/ bad   eight [ʔ] goals   eight /k/ goals
      right [ʔ] mess   right /p/ mess

Similarly, two possibilities before /j/, where the /t/ could assimilate to post-alveolar /tʃ/ or not

6.17 right [ʔ] use   right /tʃ/ use

Historically, this post-alveolar assimilation to /tʃ/ before /j/ accounts for the /tʃ/ in words like

6.18 *venture, picture, question*
and, more recently, in
situation, actual.

Many transfer this process – as for /d/ + /j/ – to the beginnings of words like

6.19 *tune, Tuesday*

(One chocolate firm recently ran a series of adverts relying on the popular perception of this tendency:

6.20 *Every day is Chooseday!)*

Note, again, that this historical instance of assimilation does not apply in US English.

Listen also for the distinction between words like *light* (with glottal stop) and *lie, right* (with glottal stop) and *rye*, etc., in these phrases

6.21	light detector	lie detector	Great Britain	grey Britain
	right bread	rye bread	hurt feelings	her feelings
	short line	shore line	tart manufacturer	tar manufacturer
	boat man	bowman		

and the subtle difference in articulation between

6.22 white shoes /'waɪʔ 'ʃuːz/ why choose /'waɪ 'tʃuːz/

Historically, the older tendency to assimilate may well account for the frequent mis-spelling of *utmost* as **upmost*. No doubt, the sense of the word and the analogy with *uppermost* also contributed. (West Walian English is again an exception, where a fully articulated /t/ is usual in all these contexts.)

*

Final /s/ and /z/ assimilate to post-alveolar /ʃ/ and /ʒ/ in the face of post-alveolar /ʃ, tʃ, dʒ/ and palatal /j/, Consider phrases with *this* /ðɪs/ and *these* /ðiːz/

6.23	this shop	/ðɪʃ 'ʃɒp/	these shops	/ðiːʒ 'ʃɒps/
	this chair	_____	these chairs	_____
	this job	_____	these jobs	_____
	this year	_____	these years	_____

Notice that in cases like *this shop, bus shelter*, there is a 'double' /ʃʃ/ to account for the /ʃ/ assimilation at the end of the first word and the /ʃ/ at the beginning of the following word.

Historically, this post-alveolar assimilation of /s, z/ before /j/ accounts for the /ʃ, ʒ/ in words like

6.24 *pressure, mission* and *pleasure, vision*
and, more recently, in
issue, usual.

It also accounts for the /ʃ/ at the beginning of words like *sure, sugar*. Notice also how /s/ readily assimilates to /ʃ/ before the /tʃ/ in words like

6.25 *mischief* /'mɪʃtʃɪf/, *question* /'kwɛʃtʃən/, *Christian* /'krɪʃtʃən/

You will have noticed how /t, d, s, z/ all yield to the post-alveolar assimilation process before /j/. This is particularly noticeable when the following word is *you* or *your*, and is easily demonstrated in the following phrases

6.26   did you?

you had your chance!

If the word *you* or *your* is unstressed (see pp. 34–35) not only does the assimilation process adjust the pronunciation of /d/ to /dʒ/ in anticipation of the /j/, but the /d/ and /j/ actually coalesce: /'dɪdʒ u/, /ju 'hædʒ ɔː 'tʃɑːns/. However if the word *you* or *your* is stressed, as, for example, in emphasis or contrast, the /j/ is retained:

6.27   /'dɪdʒ 'juː/, /'juː 'hædʒ 'jɔː 'tʃɑːns/

Notice, then, these cases where *you/your* is unstressed

6.28

I need you	/aɪ 'niːdʒ u/	I'll hide your money	/aɪ l 'haɪdʒ ɔː 'mʌni/
She loved you	_____	I've sorted your car out	_____
we'll miss you	_____	cross your arms	_____
it wakes you up	_____	he likes your sister	_____
we'll lose you	_____	use your head	_____
cocoa warms you up	_____	he sees your problem	_____
as you know	_____	This is your life	_____
as you like it	_____	does your wife know	_____
it does you good	_____	where's your money	_____
he has you in mind	_____	what was your job	_____

Remember that there are two possibilities when /t/ is followed by /j/

6.29

he'll meet you	/'miː? u/	he'll meet your friend	/'miː? jɔː/
	/'miːtʃ u/		/'miːtʃ ɔː/
it won't hurt you	_____	I hate your guts!	_____
	_____		_____

*

All the cases of assimilation we have considered so far involve an adjustment in the place of articulation in anticipation of (or in coalescence with) an immediately following consonant. The words have to belong to a phrase or a close knit syntactic structure within a clause. Assimilation often operates when a pause of hesitation interrupts the pronunciation of a phrase, like *he's gone . by bus* /...'gɒm . baɪ... / . But it does not operate when the pause realizes the boundary between two clauses: *how has he gone? By bus?* /...'gɒn . baɪ.../.

*

A quite different case of assimilation involves an adjustment in **voicing**. A voiced fricative in word-final position often loses its voicing, either partially or fully, if the next word begins with a voiceless consonant. For instance, final /v/ in *have* may weaken to a partially devoiced [v̥] before a voiceless consonant in a phrase like *have to*, or it may weaken with full devoicing and become identical to /f/. Listen to the two possibilities:

6.30   ['hæv̥ tu]   ['hæf tu]

Similarly, final /z/, e.g. *has to*

['hæz̥ tu]   ['hæs tu]

The partial devoicing process is a case of *allophonic* assimilation, but the full devoicing process amounts to *phonemic* assimilation. Notice that the /v/ of *of*, the /ð/ of *with*, the /z/ of *is, was* can all be affected.

of course [v̥, f]	with care [ð̥, θ]	he's too bad [z̥, s]
	with support [ð̥, θ]	she was fine [z̥, s]

In the following cases, note once again the tendency for a single articulation of 'double' length to account for the assimilated consonant at the end of one word and an identical consonant at the beginning of the following word.

full of fun   with thanks   that was so nice

The devoicing tendency often occurs within a word, at the juncture of two morphemes, in parallel situations. Thus *withstand* /wɪð'stænd/ becomes [wɪð̥'stænd] or /wɪθ'stænd/, and *absent* /'æbsn̩t/ becomes either ['æb̥sn̩t] or /'æpsn̩t/. Likewise *subsist, absolutely, obscene, newspaper*. In the word *absurd*, two alternative assimilation processes may be heard: either the /b/ becoming [b̥] or /p/; or the /s/ becoming /z/: /æp's3ːd/ or / æb'z3ːd /.

*

That second alternative – the voicing option – is frequently heard in other cases where a voiceless fricative, particularly /s, ʃ/, between voiced sounds becomes voiced itself. A well-known example is the change that has happened to the name *Asia*, where /ʃ/ has begun to give way to /ʒ/:

6.31   /'eɪʃə/, /'eɪʒə/; *version* /'vɜːʃən/, /'vɜːʒən/; *resource* /rɪ'sɔːs/, /rɪ'zɔːs/; *transit* /'trænsɪt/, /'trænzɪt/; *Muslim* /'mʊslɪm/ to /'mʊzlɪm/

*

These are the main cases of assimilation in English. Assimilation – phonemic or allophonic – is usually **anticipatory**: it anticipates either the adjustment in the place of articulation of final /n, d, t, s, z/ before certain consonants, or the devoicing of fricatives (and occasionally, plosives) before voiceless consonants. Assimilation is also occasionally **coalescent**: when two successive consonants affect each other as in cases like /d/ followed by /j/ as in *did you?* /'dɪdʒ u/.

But there is one other instance of assimilation in English where an adjustment is made that retains the place of articulation of a *preceding* consonant. This happens regularly in the word *happen!* If no vowel follows, the final /n/ becomes syllabic and adjusts to the bilabial articulation of /p/: /'hæpm̩/; also: *happens* /'hæpm̩z/, *happened* /'hæpm̩d/, but not in *happening*, where the /n/ is not syllabic: /'hæpnɪŋ/. Look back at p. 52. This kind of assimilation is called **retentive** or **perseverative**, and is relatively rare in English – although it is common in other languages. Other occasional instances in English include the possibility of *open* /ˈəʊpən/ becoming /ˈəʊpm̩/; *opens* /ˈəʊpənz/ becoming /ˈəʊpm̩z/ and *opened* /ˈəʊpənd/ becoming /ˈəʊpm̩d/; but *opening* /ˈəʊpnɪŋ/ keeps the non-syllabic /n/.

Elision

A second type of simplification involves not an adjustment to a sound, but its complete removal. This is known as elision; the missing sound is said to have been elided. Take the name *Christmas* as an example; it used to be a compound consisting of *Christ* and *mass*, but in the course of time, the /t/ of the first word has been elided, and nowadays nobody would normally pronounce the name with a /t/. Similarly, the word *handkerchief* used to be a compound consisting of *hand* and *kerchief*, but again in the course of time the /d/ of the first word has been elided.

As it happens, elision mainly affects final /t, d/ if they are preceded by a consonant – as in the cases above – and also followed by a word beginning with a consonant – again, as in the cases above.

First of all, we will consider the **elision of final /d/**. Notice what has happened to the /d/ in these other (formerly compound) words:

6.32　*handsome, sandwich, grandfather, grandchildren*

Notice too that as /d/ is elided in *grandparents*, the preceding /n/ is adjacent to a bilabial consonant and assimilates to /p/ by becoming /m/:

6.33　/ˈgræmˌpeərənts/

Try and transcribe:

6.34　grandpa　　　　　_____
　　　grandmother　　_____
　　　grandma　　　　_____

keeping a 'double' /m/ for the assimilating /n/ and the /m/ of the second part of the compound. Transcribe, likewise:

6.35　handbag　　　/ˈhæmˌbæg/
　　　windbag　　　_____
　　　windmill　　　_____

Transcribe

6.36　handset　　　/ˈhænˌsɛt/
　　　landscape　　_____
　　　bandstand　　_____
　　　friendship　　_____
　　　bend them　　_____

Now cases where /d/ is preceded by /l/

6.37   wild beasts   /'waɪl 'biːsts/
       old men   _____
       child protection   _____
       goldfish   _____
       fold them   _____

The fact that the elision of /d/ makes some of these words identical to others (*while, goal, foal*) does not seem to trouble native English speakers, as the context usually makes it quite clear which word is intended. Occasionally, there is potential ambiguity as in *cold shed/coal shed*, but again, usually the context is clear. Elision is sometimes expressed in 'popular' spelling, e.g. *Ol' King Cole, Ole Man River.*

Elision, however, does not take place if the following consonant is /h/, such as in

6.38   hand held   /'hænd ˌhɛld/
       grand house   _____
       wild horse   _____
       old hand   _____

and is optional if the approximants /r, w/ and /l/ follow

6.39   hand rail   _____, _____   hand luggage   _____, _____
       Grand Rapids   _____, _____   landlocked   _____, _____
       old rope   _____, _____   old lady   _____, _____
       wild west   _____, _____   wild lily   _____, _____

If /j/ follows, assimilation to /dʒ/ usually takes place

6.40   land use   /'lændʒ 'juːs/
       old year   _____

Thus, /d/ elision takes place if it is word-final, preceded by a consonant and followed immediately by a word beginning with a consonant (but with the above exceptions). It also takes place if a suffix follows which begins with the right kind of consonant. Thus /d/ is elided in *friends*, and may optionally be elided in *friendly*. What about these words?

6.41   friendship   _____
       blindness   _____
       childless   _____
       worldly   _____
       handful   _____
       child's play   _____

The past-tense suffix <-ed> is pronounced /d/ after voiced consonants other than /d/ itself (see p. 53). If the immediately following word begins with a consonant that causes elision, then the past tense suffix itself is elided. This means that the verb actually loses its tense marker; again, native English speakers do not appear to be particularly bothered by this, since there will probably be enough in the context to indicate which tense is intended. So, for example, in *I warned them*, the conditions are right for elision to take place, leaving the spoken equivalent of *I warn them*. Naturally, a person may decide to make the suffix noticeable by articulating the /d/ in an exaggerated way, but this is not normal in most ordinary, typical, informal colloquial speech. Transcribe the following as in this informal colloquial style:

6.42　I warned them　　　_____
　　　and called them　　_____
　　　and told them off　_____

*

Now, **the elision of /t/**. Just as /t/ has been elided in *Christmas,* and also in words like *castle, listen, whistle, wrestle, soften,* it is also elided in *postman, facts, vastness*. Some people, but not all, elide the /t/ in *often:* /'ɒftən, 'ɒfən/. Otherwise, it appears to parallel the case of /d/ elision, but the preceding consonant must be *voiceless* in the case of /t/ elision. Thus, /t/ is elided in

6.43　*facts*　　　　/'fæks/　　　but not in　　*faults*
　　　instincts　　/'ɪnstɪŋks/　but not in　　*intents*
　　　vastness　　'vɑːsnəs/　　but not in　　*pleasantness*

Transcribe

6.44　soft spot　　/'sɒf 'spɒt/
　　　lost cause　　_____
　　　left foot　　 _____
　　　vast spaces　_____
　　　apt remarks　_____
　　　Act Three　　_____
　　　just now　　 _____
　　　best thing　 _____

As with /d/, elision does not occur if the following consonant is /h/. Note the difference between *West Bromwich* and *West Ham*. Elision does not take place in

6.45　gift horse　　/'gɪft ˌhɔːs/
　　　guest house　_____
　　　left hand　　 _____

and is optional if the approximants /r, w/ and /l/ follow

6.46　last rites　 _____, _____　　soft landing　_____, _____
　　　left wing　 _____, _____　　gift wrap　　 _____, _____
　　　guest list　_____, _____　　wrist watch　_____, _____

If /j/ follows, either elision takes place, or assimilation to /tʃ/

6.47 last year   /'lɑːʃ jɜː/ or /'lɑːʃtʃ jɜː/

cost unit   _____, _____

lost youth   _____, _____

West Yorkshire   _____, _____

If a suffix follows which begins with the right kind of consonant, then /t/ is elided. Thus /t/ is elided in *swiftness* and may, optionally, be elided in *swiftly*. What about these words?

6.48 lifts   _____

ghostly   _____

listless   _____

softness   _____

gift's value   _____

The past tense suffix <-ed> is pronounced /t/ after voiceless consonants other than /t/ itself (see pp. 53–54). If the immediately following word begins with a consonant that causes elision, then – just like the case of /d/ – the /t/ suffix is elided. This means that in a case with past tense, like *I washed them*, where the conditions are right for elision, then it will sound exactly like the spoken equivalent of the present tense, *I wash them*. Transcribe the following in an informal colloquial style:

6.49 I left my friends   _____

crossed the street   _____

and passed the shops   _____

then lost my way   _____

Notice that /t/ does not readily get elided if it would otherwise bring two /s/s together at the end of a word:

6.50 ghosts   /'gəʊsts/

costs   _____

feasts   _____

Nevertheless, /t/ is elided in these other cases:

6.51 first serve   /'fɜːs 'sɜːv/

most surprising   _____

lost soul   _____

*

Elision, in English, mainly involves final /t, d/ when preceded by a consonant (a voiceless one in the case of /t/) and followed immediately by a word beginning with certain consonants. It also happens regularly to the /k/ of *ask* when followed immediately by any elision-inducing consonants. All the features of /t/ elision apply:

6.52 Ask me a question

He'll ask them each a question

They asked a question

Note the double elision that takes place in

They asked me a question

but /k/ is not elided if it would bring two /s/s together:

6.53   She always asks many questions

and may happen in

6.54   She'll ask loads of questions

/k/ elision is restricted to the verb *ask,* no doubt because it is used so frequently. It does not normally happen in words like *risk,* e.g. *risked,* or *task,* e.g. *task force.*

There are certain other cases of elision as a consequence of rhythm, but they will be dealt with in Chapter 7.

Epenthesis

Having considered elision – the loss of a sound – as a process of simplification, it might seem strange to consider the addition of a sound as another way of simplifying pronunciation. But there are some such cases in English.

Consider the word *young.* Its final consonant is a voiced velar nasal /ŋ/. Now consider the derived form *youngster.* You will notice that the ending begins with /s/, a voiceless alveolar fricative. The /s/ articulation is different in every respect from the /ŋ/ articulation; /s/ is voiceless, /ŋ/ is voiced; /s/ is oral, in the sense that the soft palate is raised, /ŋ/ is nasal, with the soft palate lowered; /s/ is fricative, with a partial closure in the mouth, /ŋ/ requires complete closure; and /s/ is alveolar, with the blade of the tongue against the teeth ridge, /ŋ/ is velar, with the back of the tongue against the soft palate. Thus, the transition to /s/ from /ŋ/ involves four changes: at the vocal folds, with the soft palate, with a different degree of closure with a different part of the tongue. In careful speech, it is quite possible to synchronize all these movements, but many people in ordinary, typical, informal colloquial speech do not. What happens in their case is that the changes at the vocal folds and with the soft palate are engaged first, and then the tongue 'catches up' afterwards. In other words, the transition from /ŋ/ to /s/ is staggered, with the result that an extra – transitional – sound is produced. That 'transitional' sound has the voicelessness and 'orality' of /s/ but the tongue position of the /ŋ/, and is thus identical to the articulation of the English consonant /k/.

ŋ	k	s
voiced	←	voiceless
nasal	←	oral
closed	→	fricative
velar	→	alveolar

This explains why many people, who do not synchronize all four changes, insert an additional, transitional, /k/

6.55 /ˈjʌŋkstə/

This process of adding, or inserting, an extra transitional sound is known as epenthesis.

Transcribe the word *gangster* in two ways

6.56 gangster _____ _____

A parallel process of epenthesis happens in *hamster:*

m	p	s
voiced	←	voiceless
nasal	←	oral
closed	→	fricative
bilabial	→	alveolar

Try and pronounce *hamster* in these two ways, and transcribe each

6.57 hamster _____ _____

(Epenthesis explains why *hamster* is sometimes mis-spelt as *hampster*!)

A third parallel case of epenthesis happens in *monster*. Although /n/ and /s/ share an alveolar point of articulation, the tongue changes from a flat 'broad' contact to a grooved shape. As in the other transitions, the tongue movement may lag behind, leaving the flat 'broad' contact fractionally longer; this helps to produce a transitional /t/.

n	t	s
voiced	←	voiceless
nasal	←	oral
closed	→	fricative
flat	→	grooved

Try and pronounce *monster* in these two ways, and transcribe each

6.58 monster _____ _____

This process of epenthesis in English happens whenever a nasal sound is followed by a voiceless fricative, as long as the voiceless fricative is not part of a stressed syllable.

Consider the sequence of nasal + /θ/; transcribe these words with and without appropriate epenthetic consonants

6.59 warmth _____ _____
tenth _____ _____
millionths _____ _____

length   _____   _____
strength   _____   _____

In the case of *length* and *strength,* an alternative process of simplification is possible for some speakers, the process of assimilating the /ŋ/ to /n/: /'lɛnθ/, /'strɛnθ/. But then the conditions are right again for epenthesis: /'lɛntθ/, /'strɛntθ/!

Consider also the sequence of /n/ + /s/; transcribe these words with and without epenthetic /t/

6.60   dense   _____   _____
       chance   _____   _____
       prince   _____   _____
       once   _____   _____
       patience   _____   _____

Notice then that the pronunciation with epenthetic /t/ becomes a homophone with the plural forms:

dents

chants

prints

wants

patients

a point which is not lost in jokes, e.g. about the doctor who lost his *patience/ patients*! Try *triumph, triumphal, triumphant* without, and with, epenthetic /p/. What about *circumference*?

Finally, consider the sequence of nasal + voiceless fricatives in names. The son of *Sam* is either *Samson,* or *Sampson* – with epenthetic /p/; similarly *Simson* and *Simpson, Thomson* and *Thompson.* (Not, you note, the sons of Samp, Simp and Thomp!) Epenthetic /p/ has been realized historically in the place names *Hampstead, Hampton, Hampshire, Kempton.* Epenthetic /t/ or /k/ is often pronounced (but not spelt) in names like *Benson, Hanson, Johnson, Langton, Langford.*

Liaison

Liaison is another process which involves the addition of a sound. In this case, a speaker inserts a sound in order to ease the link between vowels at the end of one word and at the beginning of an immediately following word.

The most well-known case involves a historical <r> at the end of a word. In most British ('non-rhotic') accents, the <r> in a word like *here* is not pronounced if there is either a consonant following in the next word, or silence. But if the immediately following word begins with a vowel, the <r> does get pronounced: *here in Britain* /'hɪər ɪm 'brɪtn̩/. Such an /r/ is traditionally known as a **linking /r/**, as speakers use it to *link up* the end of one word with the beginning of the next. Here are some more examples:

6.61 far   /'fɑː/   far away   /'fɑːr ə'weɪ/
     near   _____   near enough   _____
     there   _____   there inside   _____
     floor   _____   next floor up   _____
     stir   _____   stir in   _____
     ever   _____   ever after   _____
     more   _____   more examples   _____

Notice the kind of vowel that occurs in the first column: /ɑː, ɪə, ɛə, ɔə, ɜː, ə/, all relatively open or mid, and back or central/centring. It is now very common for native English speakers to add /r/ to any word ending in these vowels when the immediately following word begins with a vowel – even if there is no 'historical' /r/ in the spelling. There was, in the 1960s and 70s, a fierce controversy as to whether this 'non-historical' /r/ liaison was acceptable in standard pronunciation, but it is now widely heard and accepted as a current form, based on the analogy of the 'linking' /r/. But because of that controversy, this 'non-historical' case is usually referred to as the **intrusive /r/**. Here are some examples:

6.62 spa   /'spɑː/   the spa is open   /ðə 'spɑːr ɪz 'əʊpən/
     media   _____   media operation   _____
     law   _____   law in Scotland   _____
     milieu   _____   milieu in society _____
     Laura   _____   Laura Ashley   _____

Although the 'intrusive' /r/ is added on the analogy of the 'linking' /r/, it is basically an identical process of liaison, easing the link between two vowels across a word boundary. For some speakers, the 'intrusive' /r/ eases the boundary between morphemes even *within* a word, e.g. *drawing* may become

6.63 /'drɔːrɪŋ/

                                    *

If a word ends in the vowels /iː, i, eɪ, aɪ, ɔɪ/, some speakers use /j/ to link them to a vowel at the beginning of an immediately following word. And if a word ends in the vowels /uː, u, aʊ, əʊ/, a /w/ is often used to produce a similar link. Here are some examples:

6.64 see   siː   see off   'siːj 'ɒf
     stay   _____   stay out   _____
     high   _____   high over   _____
     toy   _____   toy animals   _____
                                       the end   _____

6.65 new   _____   new information   _____
     no   _____   no idea   _____
     how   _____   how about   _____
                                       to end   _____

Liaison with /r, j, w/ – the three approximants – eases the link between any final vowel and any vowel at the beginning of an immediately following word. It is thus another type of simplification process.

*

We have now covered all four of the processes of simplification that native speakers of English employ in ordinary, typical, informal colloquial speech. And we have transcribed plenty of examples of each type. But it must also be emphasized that this survey of simplification processes applies to English, and not necessarily to other languages. Other languages may have processes that are parallel to the English ones, but they may very likely employ fewer, or different, or more processes than English does.

Remember too, native speakers have the option of **not** employing these simplification processes, especially in a slow, deliberate style. Imagine, for instance, the opening announcement at a seminar.

6.66   Today our subject is Anne Boleyn   /...ˈæn bʊˈlɪn/

and compare it with a less formal style in a following statement of explanation

6.67   As you know, Anne Boleyn /ˈæm bʊˈlɪn/ was Henry VIII's second wife

Transcribe these names and places in this less formal style		
6.68 Dan Brown	David Beckham	Liz Yates
John Paul	David Cameron	Roger Ellis
John Milton	Bertrand Russell	Barbara Edwards
Catherine Cookson	Ronald Reagan	Leeds United
Don Quixote	Raymond Baxter	West Virginia
Ryan Giggs	Old Trafford	Rift Valley *(See Key)*

We have now covered every angle of the transcription of words in English!

II . . . and Discourse

7 Rhythm

Talk does not normally consist of single words. Sometimes it does, but much more often, talk consists of a vast number of words connected together in phrases, clauses, sentences, phonological paragraphs – in whole texts of discourse. An utterance that consists of a single word is usually a response like *Yes, No, Well, Maybe, OK, Certainly, Absolutely,* or *Tench, Paul, Cardiff, British, Male* . . . But in most talk, words pile upon each other and they affect the pronunciation of each other. We have seen some of the effects of words coming together in phrases in Chapter 6. But there is another kind of effect when words come together in phrases and clauses. Just as words have a stress pattern, phrases and clauses do too as they become part of real discourse.

Think again of the old song:

Ten green bottles
Hanging **on** the **wall**
And if **one green bott**le
Should **acciden**tally **fall**
There'd be **nine green bott**les
Hanging **on** the **wall**

Each line has three beats, or stresses (printed in bold) which means that certain words and syllables are pronounced *without* stress (printed plain). In order to say these unstressed words quickly enough not to spoil the rhythm, they are usually pronounced with a weak vowel. And this means that certain words have at least two possible pronunciations – a strong form with a strong vowel, and a weak form with a weak vowel. Take the word *and* for example. Taken by itself, it is pronounced as /ˈænd/; this is its strong form. And it is sometimes pronounced like that in talk, for emphasis or contrast. But much more often, it is pronounced in a different way, as in this song, as /ən/; this is its weak form. The choice between its strong or weak form depends upon its role in an utterance; if it is just connecting words or clauses, it is usually pronounced in its weak form, but if someone wants to draw attention to the connection itself, it would be pronounced in its strong form. This is a choice at the level of discourse which is then reflected in the degree of prominence that a person gives a word within a phrase or clause. As a general rule, lexical (or 'content') words like nouns, verbs, adjectives and adverbs are made prominent because of their importance in a message, whereas grammatical (or 'structure') words like conjunctions, prepositions, pronouns, determiners and auxiliary and modal verbs are usually pronounced without any prominence because their role is basically to provide structure to phrases and clauses in utterances. English rhythm, then, relates to the way in which unstressed syllables are integrated with the strong syllables of prominent words in discourse, to produce the pronunciation of phrases and clauses.

Most talk is conducted in an informal, rather rapid, colloquial style. Occasionally, talk is slow and formal, in which case the processes of simplification would not necessarily operate. Sometimes, the pace of talk is reduced to dictation speed when even rhythm choices do not operate. If you had to dictate the *Ten Green Bottles* song, you would probably articulate all the words in their full forms. (The dots (.) indicate pausing.)

7.1 'tɛn . 'griːn . 'bɒt̩z
'hæŋɪŋ . 'ɒn . 'ðə . 'wɔːl
'ænd . ɪf . 'wʌn . 'griːn . 'bɒt̩
'ʃʊd . æksi . 'dɛntəli . 'fɔːl
'ðɛə . wʊd . 'biː . 'naɪn . 'griːn . 'bɒt̩ z
'hæŋɪŋ . 'ɒn . 'ðə . 'wɔːl

Contrast this pronunciation with the way you would probably sing it!

7.2 'tɛŋ 'griːm 'bɒt̩ z
'hæŋɪŋ 'ɒn ðə 'wɔːl
ən ɪf 'wʌŋ 'griːm 'bɒt̩
ʃəd 'æksɪ'dɛntli 'fɔːl
ðə b bi 'naɪŋ 'griːm 'bɒt̩ z
'hæŋɪŋ 'ɒn ðə 'wɔːl

Obviously, normal, ordinary, informal, colloquial talk is not like singing with its carefully measured beat, but it is nevertheless marked by rhythm choices and simplification processes as illustrated in the song.

So, just as words have stress patterns, so do phrases and clauses. Indeed, some words and phrases have identical patterns, for instance *inaction* and *in action* /ɪnˈækʃən/, even *indeed* and *in deed* /ɪnˈdiːd/. Listen:

7.3 /ɪnˈækʃən/, /ɪnˈdiːd/

In our practice of the effects of rhythm in the pronunciation of discourse in English, we will concentrate on the grammatical items and begin with the prepositions.

Prepositions

Prepositions have full forms and weak forms. Strong forms are used for emphasis or contrast and when they occur at the ends of clauses:

7.4 where are you flying to /tuː/
and travelling from /frɒm/
which hotel are you staying at /æt/
how long are you going for /fɔː/

But in ordinary prepositional phrases, they are usually unstressed.

7.5 I'm flying to /tə/ Glasgow
on /ɒm/ Monday
from /frəm/ Gatwick
with /wɪð/ a budget airline
staying at /ət/ the 'Old Barn'
in /ɪn/ in the city centre
for /fə/ the weekend

Notice that the vowel in some prepositions changes to a weak vowel, like *from* /frəm/ and *at* /ət/, but in others like *on, with, in* it does not. In the case of *to*, the vowel changes to the neutral vowel if a consonant follows immediately, or to the weak vowel /tu/ before a vowel. Look back at p. 34. In the case of *for*, the vowel changes to the neutral vowel, but a linking /r/ is added as liaison before a following vowel. Now try these examples

7.6 flying to _____ San Francisco
from _____ Birmingham
staying at _____ the 'Old Castle'
for _____ two weeks

7.7 flying to _____ LA (/'ɛl 'eɪ/)
from _____ Manchester
staying at _____ the 'Old Lodge'
for _____ a few days

The preposition *of* has a strong form: /ɒʌ/ for emphasis, contrast and the end position of a clause, e.g.

7.8 what's he thinking of /ɒʌ/
and a weak form when unstressed /əv/

7.9 thinking of /əv/ his holidays
Transcribe

7.10 what does his plan consist of _____
a week of _____ sun in the south of _____ Spain, then climb to the top of _____ the Rock of _____ Gibraltar, then a month of _____ hiking along the coast of _____ North Africa.

The weak form is also often pronounced with /v/ elided, reducing it to /ə/. Historically, this is what has happened in telling the time, e.g. *2 o'clock* /'tuː ə'klɒk/ for the older *2 of (the) clock*. It is also what has happened in phrases like *a cup of tea* becoming *a cuppa* /ˈkʌpə /. An old advert to encourage the drinking of milk was

Drinka
Pinta (= a pint of)
Milka
Day

Popular spellings of *kind of* and *sort of* as *kinda, sorta* display the same observation.

7.11   you sort of /ˈsɔːt ə/ try
it's kind of /ˈkaɪnd ə/ nice

Transcribe the following according to whether /əʌ/ or /ə/ is used

7.12   a cup of _____ coffee at 11 o'_____ clock
a cup of _____ tea at 4 o'_____ clock
a pint of _____ beer at 8 o' _____ clock
a packet of _____ crisps at the end of _____ the day

None of the other prepositions have special weak forms with a change of vowel; they are transcribed with a stress mark if stressed, and without it if unstressed.

7.13   we're going through /θruː/ France
he said We're going *through* /ˈθruː/ France, not *to* /ˈtuː/ France
and we're going for /fə/ two weeks, not *in* /ˈɪn/ two weeks.
and you need to check your passport *before* /bɪˈfɔː/, not *after* /ˈɑːftə/.

Transcribe

7.14   single to ___ Liverpool please
the 8.25 for _____ Manchester will be leaving from _____Platform 1
change at ___ Crewe for _____ all stations to __ Liverpool Lime Street
we apologize that there'll be a delay of __ ten minutes.

*

Conjunctions

The most common conjunction is **and**. As we have already noted, its full form is /ˈænd/ and its most frequent weak form is /ən/. The /n/ of its weak form is vulnerable to the process of assimilation, as in *bed and breakfast*

7.15   /ˈbɛb m̩ ˈbrɛkfəst/

Transcribe *and* in these orders for breakfast

7.16   fruit and _____ breakfast cereals
muesli and _____ cornflakes
eggs and _____ bacon

toast and _____ marmalade

tea and _____ coffee

If you order *ham and egg*, note that you might possibly retain the /d/: either /ən/ or /ənd/. What about

7.17   grapefruit and ____ (or ____) orange?

If the conditions are right, the /n/ may give way to a syllabic /n̩/ (or /m̩/, as in *bed and breakfast*, or /ŋ̍/). Transcribe *and* in these suggestions for lunch

7.18   bread and cheese   _____   soup and bread   _____

omelette and chips   _____   roast pork and gravy   _____

cake and cream   _____

*

The conjunction **or** usually remains unchanged when unstressed, except in a few set phrases. When a genuine choice or alternative is being offered, the conjunction remains as /ɔː/ with the possibility of /r/ liaison as in

7.19   eat in or /ɔːr/ out

Notice the full form in

7.20   brown bread or ___ white

tea or ___ coffee

with or ___ without

but in set phrases like *one or two,* the conjunction may be reduced to /ə/. Compare
(How long are you staying?)

7.21   two or /ə/ three days

well, is it two *or* /'ɔː/ three days

well, when we've more or /ə/ less finished

Similarly, with *nor.*

7.22   he's not staying, and nor /'nɔːr/ are you

a day or /ə/ two is neither here nor /nə/ there

*

The conjunction **but** /bʌt/ is weakened to /bət/ when unstressed. In these it is unstressed:

7.23   the weather will be dry but /bət/ cold

wet but _____ mild

warm at first, but _____ cold later

you should be all right, but _____ take an umbrella just in case

But is stressed when a speaker wants to emphasize a contrast:

7.24 you should be all right, *but* _____ take an umbrella just in case

*

The conjunction *as* /æz/ is weakened to /əz/ when unstressed:

7.25 they were as /əz/ snug as _____ a bug in a rug
               as _____ warm as _____ toast
               as _____ dry as _____ possible

The /z/ is susceptible to the process of assimilation:

take as _____ much as _____ you like

If *you* in this context is unstressed, the /j/ will be elided: /əʒ u/: but if *you* is stressed, the /j/ is retained: . . . as *you* think best.

7.26 /... əʒ ˈjuː/

As at the beginning of an utterance is usually strong:

7.27 as /ˈæz/ I came to work today

*

The conjunction ***because*** has a strong form /bɪˈkɒz/ and a weak form when unstressed: /bɪkəz/. At the beginning of an utterance, it is usually strong:

7.28 because /bɪˈkɒz/ it's raining, we'll stay inside

7.29 we can go out, because /bɪkəz/ it's stopped

The weak form can be further weakened to a single syllable: /kəz/, popularly spelt as *cos*:

7.30 let's go out, cos /kəz/ it's stopped raining
      The final /z/ is susceptible to the process of assimilation:

7.31 we're going out, cos /kəʒ/ you said we could
      (The /j/ of *you* would be elided if unstressed.)

The weak forms of *because* are valid too in the phrasal preposition *because of*.

7.32 we stayed in because /bɪkəz/ of /əv/ the rain
      we stayed in cos /kəz/ of /əv/ the rain

*

The word *that* is usually pronounced in a weak form /ðət/ when it operates as a relative pronoun or conjunction, as in

7.33 the weather that /ðət/ was forecast
      they said that _____ it would be wet
      now that _____ it's stopped . . .

The word *that* is usually pronounced in its strong form /ˈðæt/ as a demonstrative adjective or pronoun:

7.34   it rained throughout that /ˈðæt/ day
       so that /ˈðæt / was that /ˈðæt/
       it was that /ˈðæt/ wet

Transcribe

7.35   that _____ man said that _____ all that _____ rain that _____ fell yesterday
       was enough to fill that _____ reservoir that _____ we saw.

⋆

Finally, the conjunction ***than*** has a strong form /ˈðæn/, but is usually pronounced in its weak form /ˈðən/:

7.36   wetter than /ˈðən/ yesterday
       more rain than _____ ever
       rather go abroad than _____ stay here

⋆

None of the other conjunctions have special weak forms with a change of vowel; they are transcribed with a stress mark if they are stressed, and without it if unstressed:

7.37   I said *if* /ˈɪf/
       if /ɪf/ you like

7.38   *while* /ˈwaɪl/ it's raining let's play Monopoly
       let's play Monopoly while /waɪl/ it's raining

⋆

Determiners

The determiners that have special weak forms are the definite and indefinite articles and the possessive adjectives.

The definite article *the* has a special strong form: /ˈðiː/, as in

7.39   Spain is the /ˈðiː/ place for the sun
       It also has an ordinary strong form: /ˈðə/ as in

7.40   the definite article is *the* /ˈðə/

       (This is one of only two occasions in SESP when the neutral vowel is stressed.) *The* also has two weak forms in most accents, though the second is less common in General American: /ðə/ before consonants, /ði/ before vowels, as in

       The /ðə/ definite article
       The /ði/ articles

Transcribe the following:

7.41   the weather   _____   the umbrella   _____
       the rain   _____   the ice   _____
       the morning   _____   the afternoon _____
       the night   _____   the evening   _____
       the hotel   _____   the hour   _____
       the usual   _____   the unusual   _____

*

The indefinite articles have strong forms: /eɪ/ before consonants, /æn/ before vowels.

7.42   I said *an* /ˈæn/ egg, not half a dozen!

7.43   at least you've *a* /ˈeɪ/ drink, even if it's not what you ordered

The corresponding weak forms are /ə/ and /ən/.
Transcribe

7.44   a coffee   _____   an ice cream   _____
       a banana   _____   an apple   _____
       a hostel   _____   an inn   _____
       a useful thing _____   an ugly scene _____

*

The word **some** is used for indefiniteness with mass nouns like *milk*. Its strong form is /sʌm/ and its weak form is /səm/.

7.45   at least you've got *some* /ˈsʌm/ milk
       I need some /səm/ more milk

Transcribe these phrases with both the strong and the weak forms:

7.46   some sugar   _____ , _____ _____
       some money   _____ , _____ _____
       some change   _____ , _____ _____
       some time   _____ , _____ _____

*

Any and **many** have the same form in both stressed and unstressed situations:

7.47   I haven't had *any* /ˈɛni/ sugar
       I haven't had any /ɛni/ *sugar*

7.48   they've been *many* /ˈmɛni / times
       I do not have many /mɛni / *ideas*

But there is the possibility of weak forms in common phrases: /əni/ and /məni/ as in

7.49 I haven't any /əni/ left
how many /məni/ do you need

*

The **demonstrative adjectives** are *this* /ðɪs/, *that* /ðæt/, *these* /ðiːz/ and *those* /ðəʊz/. They do not change in unstressed positions: it is in this respect that it is important to distinguish between *that* as a conjunction which regularly weakens to /ðət/ and *that* as a determiner that retains its strong form.

Notice how the final /s/ of *this,* and the final /z/ of *these* and *those* are susceptible to the process of assimilation:

7.50 what are you going to do with all those /ðəʊʒ/ euros? and this ____ cheque?

*

The **possessive adjectives** are *my* /maɪ/, *your* /jɔː/, *his* /hɪz/, *her* /hɜː/, *its* /ɪts/, *our* /aʊə/, *their* /ðɛə/ and *whose* /huːz/. Strong forms are used for emphasis or contrast.

My and *their* do not normally have a weak form:

7.51 hey, that's *my* /'maɪ/ sun cream, *my* ____ towel, *my* ____ place

7.52 now, let me think. I've got my /maɪ/ *wallet*, my ____ *passport*, my ____
ticket _____ and my ____ *insurance*.

Our is often weakened to /ɑː/ (look back at p. 71), and with /r/ liaison:

7.53 we're off on our /ɑː/ holidays on our /ɑːr/ old bikes

Your is often weakened to /jə/, with /r/ liaison – hence its popular spelling as *yer*:

7.54 off on your /jə/ holidays?
on your /jə/ bike? on your /jər/ own?

His, her and *whose* have weak forms with /h/ elision if immediately preceded by a word:

7.55 what's his /ɪz/ name? I don't know his /ɪz/ name
what's her /ɜː/ name? I don't know her /ɜː/ name
the couple whose /uz/ names I've forgotten

If they begin a new utterance, the /h/ is usually pronounced.

7.56 whose /huːz/ tickets are these?
his /hɪz/ name is Paolo
her /hɜː/ name is Michaela

*

Titles

Most titles are stressed:

7.57   Mr /'mɪstə/ Smith   Mr /'mɪstər/ Evans
       Mrs /'mɪsɪz/ Smith   Mrs /'mɪsɪʒ/ Jones
       Miss /'mɪs/ Smith   Miss /'mɪʃ/ Jones
       Ms /'məz/ Smith   Ms /'məʒ/ Jones
       (NB the only other occasion for stressed /'ə/. Look back at p. 111.)
       Master /'mɑːstə/ Tom   Master /'mɑːstər/ Edward
       Baroness /'bærənəʃ/ Young
       President /'prɛzɪdn̩t/ Obama
       Queen /'kwiːn/ Elizabeth
       Prince /'prɪns, 'prɪnts/ Philip

but some other monosyllabic titles are often unstressed:

7.58   St /sənt/ Andrew
       Sir /sə/ Winston   Sir /sər/ Anthony

*

Pronouns

The subject pronouns are *I* /aɪ/, *you* /juː /, *he* /hiː/, *she* /ʃiː/, *it* /ɪt/, *we* /wiː/ and *they* /ðeɪ/; the object pronouns, where different, are *me* /miː/, *him* /hɪm/, *her* /hɜː/, *us* /ʌs/ and *them* /ðɛm/. The relative pronouns are *who* /huː/, and, possibly, *whom* /huːm/; and the possessive pronouns are *mine* /maɪn/, *yours* /jɔːz/, *his* /hɪz/, *hers* /hɜːz/, *ours* /aʊəz/ (or /ɑːz/), *theirs* /ðɛəz/ and *whose* /huːz/. These strong forms are used for emphasis or contrast; there are weak forms for many of them in unstressed positions. However, the possessive pronouns are not normally used in unstressed positions.

The weak forms of *he, she, we, me* all take a weak vowel:

7.59   he /hi/ told me /mi/, so we /wi/ know she /ʃi/ *is* going to Spain

The weak forms of *us* and *them* take the neutral vowel

7.60   they told us /əs/ that you saw them /ðəm/ on their way

A special case arises with *let's* /lɛts/ as distinct from *let us* /lɛt əs/. Compare

7.61   *let's go, let us go*

The weak forms of *he, him, her* and *who* tend to allow /h/ elision unless they begin a new utterance, like *his, her, whose* (see p. 113).

7.62   he /hi/ has heard, but does he /i/ understand?
       well, I told him /ɪm/
       will he /i/ let her /ɜː/ know
       she's the one who /u/ will understand

You, is weakened to /ju/ or even – like *your* – to /jə/, especially in comment phrases like *you know, you see*; but also consider

7.63   are you /jə/ going today?
we'll see you /jə/ there

The /j/ is susceptible to coalescence immediately after /t, d/:

7.64   we'll meet /ˈmiːtʃ ə/ you there
we'll need you /ˈniːdʒ ə/ there
did you /ˈdɪdʒ ə/ go
must you /ˈmʌʃtʃ u/

*

Finally, there is the pronoun **one**

7.65   /wʌn, wɒn/

In an unstressed position, it generally keeps its strong form:

One /wʌn, wɒn/ *must not lose one's* /wʌnz, wɒnz/ *head, must one* /wʌn, wɒn/

I'd like one /wʌn, wɒn/ of the red ones /wʌnz, wɒnz/

There is a weak form that is occasionally used: /ən/, popularly spelled as *'un*

7.66   the little uns /ənz/

*

Auxiliary verbs

The auxiliary verbs *be, have* and *do* and their various forms are used in verb phrases to indicate aspect, emphasis and contrast, and to operate negative and interrogative functions. There are strong forms and weak forms for each verb. Each of these verbs also acts as a full, lexical verb, in which case, they will normally be pronounced in their strong forms, e.g.

7.67   To be /ˈbiː/ or not to be /ˈbiː/
To have /ˈhæv/ and to hold
To do /ˈduː/ or die

As auxiliary verbs, they are stressed for emphasis or contrast, but are unstressed otherwise:

7.68   To see and *be* /ˈbiː/ seen   You *won't* be /bi/ seen

7.69   To fight and to *have* /ˈhæv/ fought   You *must* have /əv/ fought

7.70   *Do* /ˈduː/ take a seat   *Where* do /du/ I sit?

*

Be

7.71   I *am* /ˈæm/ going

      Am is weakened to /əm/ after a consonant, e.g.

7.72   where am /əm/ I staying?

      and to /m/ after a vowel, e.g.

7.73   I'm /m/ staying here

7.74   you *are* /ˈɑː/ going

      with /r/ liaison:

      you *are* /ˈɑːr/ invited

      Are is weakened to /ə/, e.g.

7.75   *all* the boys are /ə/ going

      with /r/ liaison, e.g.
      all the boys are /ər/ invited

      Are may be weakened to /r/ following a vowel:

7.76   you're invited /jɔː r, jə r/
      they're invited /ðeɪ r, ðɛə r/

7.77   he *is* /ˈɪz/ going

      Is is weakened in a way parallel to the morphological variations of the <-es>
      inflection (look back at pp. 53–54)

7.78   James is /ɪz/ going, and Janice is /ɪz/ too   (/ɪz, əz/ after sibilants)
      John's /z/ going, and Claire's /z/ thinking about it   (/z/ after other voiced
      sounds)
      Jack's /s/ going, but Elizabeth's /s/ not   (/s/ after voiceless sounds)

7.79   he *was* /ˈwɒz/ going

      Was is weakened to /wəz/:

7.80   Sarah was /wəz/ going too, and so was /wəʒ/ Judith

7.81   they *were* /ˈwɜː/ going

      Were is weakened to /wə/, with possible /r/ liaison:

7.82   none of them were /wə/ going, even though they were /wər/ all invited

7.83   I've *been* /ˈbiːn/ invited already

      Been is weakened to /bɪn/:

7.84   just think, we've *all* been /bɪn/ invited

*

Have

7.85 I *have* /ˈhæv/ seen it
she *has* /ˈhæz/ seen it
they *had* /ˈhæd/ seen it

Have, has, had 'suffer' /h/ elision in their weak forms unless they begin new utterances:

7.86 have /həv/ *you* seen it
has /həz / *he* seen it
had /həd/ *they* seen it

Otherwise the weak forms retain the neutral vowel after a consonant, but lose it after a vowel:

7.87 yes, I ve /v/ seen it, and the boys ve /əv/ seen it too
yes, he s /z/ seen it, and Janice s /əz/ seen it too
yes, they d /d/ seen it, and the girls d /əd/ seen it too

Has also follows the morphological variations of the <-es> inflection, like *is:*

7.88 James s gone /əz/
John s gone /z/
Jack s gone /s/

*

Do

7.89 I *do* /ˈduː/ believe in God

Do is weakened to /du/ or /də/:

7.90 do /du, də/ *they* believe in God
do /du, də/ *you* believe too

7.91 she *does* /ˈdʌz/ believe in God

Does is weakened to /dəz/:

7.92 does /dəz/ *he* believe too

Note that in *do you* /də ju/, the neutral vowel is often elided, allowing a process of coalescent assimilation to take place: /dju/ becomes /dʒu/ (or /dʒə/).

7.93 how do you do? /ˈhaʊ dʒə ˈduː/
what do you think? /ˈwɒt dʒə ˈθɪŋk/
do you *really* believe /dʒu ˈrɪəli bəˈliːv/

Modal verbs

Modal verbs add degrees of a sense of likelihood, necessity and possibility to the verb phrase. They include

can /kæn/ and could /kʊd/
may /meɪ/ and might /maɪt/
shall /ʃæl/ and should /ʃʊd/
will /wɪl/ and would /wʊd/
must /mʌst/ and ought /ɔːt/

They are pronounced in these full forms when stressed, especially for emphasis or contrast:

7.94 can /ˈkæn/ you speak Spanish? I can /ˈkæn/ and I will /ˈwɪl/
but what about Catalan? I would /ˈwʊd/ if I could /ˈkʊd/

May, *might* and *ought* do not have special weak forms when unstressed, but the other modal verbs do.

7.95 she can /kən/ speak Spanish quite well
she could /kəd/ have said that in Spanish for you
we shall /ʃəl/ see if she can /ˈkæn/
they should /ʃəd/ tell her to come
how will /wəl/ they know you're going
we would /wəd/ have to tell them
she must /məst/ at least be given a chance
yes, she must /məs/ be given the chance at least

Will and *shall* are both regularly reduced to /l/ or /əl/; and *would* and *should* to /d/ or /əd/; thus the semantic differences between them are lost.

7.96 we'll /l/ see you tonight
if she'd /d/ talk in Spanish, that'd /əd/ help us a lot
otherwise Paul'll /əl/ try

Final /d/ of *could*, *should*, *would* and *had*, like *did*, is susceptible to the processes of assimilation.

7.97 they *could* /ˈkʊg/ go, if they could /kəb/ manage *without* her
they *should* /ˈʃʊb/ be able to manage
they *would* /ˈwʊb/ be able to manage if she went with them
she'd /g/ go *with* them, but *would* you /ˈwʊdʒ u/ let her
had you /ˈhædʒ u/ thought of going yourself
how would you /wədʒ ə/ feel about that

*

Just, not, so, there

The first three of these words figure regularly in all kinds of phrases and idioms, and no doubt it is because of their frequency that they have acquired weak forms, in addition to their strong forms

7.98 they've *just* /ˈdʒʌst/ arrived, *just* /ˈdʒʌs/ this minute
not /ˈnɒt/ bad, but they'll be *so* /ˈsəʊ/ tired

7.99   oh, we're not so /sə/ bad, thank you
       we weren't /'wɜːnt/ held up anywhere
       just /dʒəs/ glad to be back

There has a special weak form in existential clauses, in contrast to locative senses:

7.100 it was nice being *there* /'ðɛə/, but *there*'s /ðə z/ no place like home

There is a further complication in the pronunciation of *n't*. We have already noted that final /t/ is now often articulated as a glottal stop [ʔ] before any immediately following consonant (except /h/). This would account for

7.101 I don't know /aɪ 'dəʊnt[ʔ] 'nəʊ/

The [ʔ] would, however, not prevent the processes of assimilation operating in informal colloquial speech, so these alternatives exist:

7.102 I don't believe it   /aɪ 'dəʊnt[ʔ] bə'liːv ɪt/ or /aɪ 'dəʊmp bə'liːv ɪt/
       I don't get it   /aɪ 'dəʊnt[ʔ] 'gɛt ɪt/ or /aɪ 'dəʊŋk 'gɛt ɪt/
       why don't you   /waɪ 'dəʊnt[ʔ] ju/ or /waɪ 'dəʊntʃ u/

The same kind of alternative pronunciations operate with

aren't: we aren't going	/wi 'ɑːnt[ʔ] gəʊɪŋ/ or /wi 'ɑːŋk gəʊɪŋ/
isn't: it isn't possible	/ɪt 'ɪzənt[ʔ] 'pɒsɪbəl/ or /ɪt 'ɪzəmp 'pɒsɪbəl/
wasn't: he wasn't paying	/hi 'wɒzn̩t[ʔ] 'peɪɪŋ/ or /hi wɒzəmp 'peɪɪŋ/
weren't: we weren't kept	/wi 'wɜːnt[ʔ] kɛpt/ or /wi 'wɜːŋk kɛpt/
haven't: they haven't paid	/ðeɪ 'hævənt[ʔ] 'peɪd/ or / eɪ 'hævəmp 'peɪd/
hasn't: she hasn't complained	/ʃi 'hæzn̩t[ʔ] kəm'pleɪnd/or /ʃi 'hæzəŋk k.../
hadn't: it hadn't come	/ɪt 'hædn̩t[ʔ] kʌm/ or /ɪt hægŋk kʌm/
doesn't: he doesn't know	/hi 'dʌzn̩t[ʔ] nəʊ/ or /hi 'dʌzŋ̩ʔ nəʊ/
didn't: I didn't believe him	/aɪ 'dɪdn̩t[ʔ] bə'liːv ɪm/ or /aɪ 'dɪbmp bə'liːv ɪm/
can't: I can't be bothered	/aɪ 'kɑːnt[ʔ] bi 'bɒðəd/ or /aɪ 'kɑːmp bi 'bɒðəd/
couldn't: he couldn't be	/hi 'kʊdn̩t[ʔ] bi/ or /hi 'kʊbm̩p bi/
shan't: we shan't go	/wi 'ʃɑːnt[ʔ] gəʊ/ or /wi 'ʃɑːŋk gəʊ/
shouldn't: you shouldn't go	/ju 'ʃʊdn̩t[ʔ] gəʊ/ or /ju 'ʃʊgŋk gəʊ/
won't: you won't make it	/ju 'wəʊnt[ʔ] 'meɪk ɪt/ or /ju 'wəʊmp 'meɪk ɪt/
wouldn't: they wouldn't mind	/ðeɪ 'wʊdn̩t[ʔ] 'maɪnd/ or /ðeɪ 'wʊbmp 'maɪnd/
mustn't: you mustn't come	/ju 'mʌsn̩t[ʔ] 'kʌm/ or /ju 'mʌʃəŋk 'kʌm/
mightn't: he mightn't care	/hi 'maɪtn̩t[ʔ] kɛə/ or /hi 'maɪtŋ'k kɛə/
oughtn't: they oughtn't to	/ðeɪ 'ɔːtn̩t[ʔ] tu/
needn't: you needn't bother	/ju 'niːdn̩t[ʔ] 'bɒðə/ or /ju 'niːbmp 'bɒðə/
daren't: she daren't move	/ʃi 'dɛənt[ʔ] 'muːv/ or /ʃi 'dɛəmp 'muːv/

If this wasn't complicated enough, it is also observable how people are simplifying some of these phrases even further. If the *n't* follows a vowel, the /n/ can change to a nasalization of that vowel and the /t/ to a glottal stop.

7.103   I don't ['dɔ̃ʊ̃ʔ] know
I can't ['kɑ̃ːʔ] believe it
they aren't ['ɑ̃ːʔ] going
we weren't ['wɜ̃ːʔ] coming
we shan't ['ʃɑ̃ːʔ] go
you won't ['wɔ̃ʊ̃ʔ] make it
she daren't ['dɛ̃ɜ̃ʔ] move

Finally, to add yet further to these complications, people very often simplify in another way by eliding the /t/ of *n't,* even though it is preceded by a voiced sound /n/:

7.104   I don't know   /aɪ 'dəʊn 'nəʊ/ or even /aɪ də 'nəʊ/ (= I 'dunno')
I don't care   /aɪ 'dəʊŋ 'kɛə/
we won't bother   /wi 'wəʊm 'bɒðə/
you didn't say   /ju 'dɪdn̩ 'seɪ/
etc.

A similar process of elision explains how *want to* and *going to* get pronounced:

7.105   I want to go (I 'wanna' go)   /aɪ 'wɒnə 'gəʊ/
I'm going to go (I'm gonna go)   /aɪm 'gɒnə 'gəʊ/

To summarize this complex range of possibilities, cases of *n't* immediately after a vowel (as in *aren't, weren't, don't, can't, won't, shan't, daren't*) can be pronounced as follows:

Don't talk: /'dəʊnt[tʰ]/, /'dəʊnt[ʔ]/, ['dɔ̃ʊ̃ʔ], /'dəʊn/
Don't push   /'dəʊnt[tʰ]/, /'dəʊmp/, ['dɔ̃ʊ̃ʔ], /'dəʊm/
Don't go   /'dəʊnt[tʰ]/, /'dəʊŋk/, ['dɔ̃ʊ̃ʔ], /'dəʊŋ/

Most of these possibilities are also valid for other words ending in /-nt/: however, the /t/ element is usually retained whether it is realized as [t] or [ʔ] or assimilated:

pleasantness   /'plɛzənt[ʔ]nəs/
resentment   /rɪ'zɛnt[ʔ]mənt, rɪ'zɛmpmənt/
pleasant places   /'plɛzn̩t[ʔ], 'plɛzəmp 'pleɪʃəz/
recent case   /'riːsn̩t[ʔ], 'riːsəŋk 'keɪsəz/
front page   /'frʌnt[ʔ], 'frʌmp/ ~ ['frʌ̃ʔ] /'peɪdʒ/
front cover   /'frʌnt[ʔ], 'frʌŋk/ ~ ['frʌ̃ʔ] /'kʌvə/

In all these cases of *n't* and final *-nt,* you have to listen carefully to what is actually said; and being aware of the various possibilities will help to discern that. In such cases, it seems worth while transcribing a glottal stop as such, [ʔ], even though, strictly speaking, it does not belong to broad (phonemic) transcriptions.

Syllable elision in lexical items and phrases

The pressure from rhythm accounts not only for the proliferation of special weak forms of many grammatical items but also for the elimination of whole syllables, especially in verb phrases with auxiliary and modal verbs. Thus in

I don't know if he's coming

the two syllables of *do not* are reduced to one, *don't,* and also the two syllables of *he is* to one, *he's.*

There has been a similar strong tendency to eliminate syllables in lexical items too, specially where there is a succession of unstressed syllables separated by /r, l, n /. Typically, the unstressed vowel is elided before such a consonant; in this way the syllable sequence is reduced. Thus historically, *history* has changed from /ˈhɪstəri/ to /ˈhɪstri/ in most – but not all – British accents, and *secretary* from /ˈsɛkrətəri/, or /ˈsɛkrətɛəri/, to /ˈsɛkrətri/. Here is a sample list of ordinary words with unstressed <-ar->, <-er->, <-or->, <-our-> and <-ur-> which gets eliminated before another unstressed syllable.

7.106		7.107		7.108		7.109	
stationary		stationery		category		natural	
/ˈsteɪʃənri/		/ˈsteɪʃənri/		/ˈkætəgri/		/ˈnætʃrəl/	
secretary		every		factory		century	
primary		grocery		sensory		luxury	
secondary		delivery		memory		
tertiary				advisory		
quandary		Everest				
ordinary		interest		temporal		neighbouring
				doctoral		flavouring
estuary		average				
sanctuary		coverage				favourable
January		camera		motoring		favourite
		opera		monitoring		
		general		glamorous		
		generous		humorous		
		generative				
		delivering				
		suffering				

Notice how the four syllables of *February* /ˈfɛbruəri/ get reduced to three: /ˈfɛbrəri, ˈfɛbjəri/, and even to two /ˈfɛbri/.

7.110   February

Similarly, *library, literary, temporary* are sometimes reduced with the loss of one /r/:

7.111   /ˈlaɪbri/, /ˈlɪtri/, /ˈtɛmpri/.

There is, however, usually no reduction in those words where otherwise /l/ and /r/ would come together:

7.112   salary /ˈsæləri/; celery /ˈsɛləri/; calorie /ˈkæləri/; colouring /ˈkʌlərɪŋ/

not */ˈsælri/, etc.

American practice is to give a secondary stress to the <a> in words like *primary, secondary*; and primary stress in derived adverbs; many British follow this pattern in the adverbs: thus *primarily* is either

7.113   /ˈpraɪmrəli/ or /praɪˈmɛrəli/ or /praɪˈmɛərəli/ or /praɪˈmærəli/.

Listen and transcribe theses words

7.114   secondarily, temporarily

_____   _____   _____   _____

A similar kind of reduction takes place where two unstressed syllables are separated by /l/. Thus, older *historically* /hɪsˈtɒrɪkəli/ loses the syllable before /l/: /hɪsˈtɒrɪkli/. Transcribe

7.115   technically   _____
        scientifically   _____
        economically   _____
        politically   _____
        musically   _____

A similar loss happens in words like this: *carefully* /ˈkɛəfəli/ becomes /ˈkɛəfli/. Transcribe

7.116   hopefully   _____
        helpfully   _____
        joyfully   _____
        usefully   _____
        woefully   _____

It also happens in this word: *easily* /ˈiːzili/ becomes /ˈiːzli/, and also in words like this: *usually* /ˈjuːʒuəli/ becomes /ˈjuːʒəli/ or even /ˈjuːʒli/. Transcribe in these two colloquial styles

7.117   actually   _____   _____
        casually   _____   _____

The words *chocolate* and *family* are both regularly reduced to two syllables: /ˈtʃɒklət/; /ˈfæmli/, and verbs with an unstressed syllable with /l/ in final position, followed by the *–ing* suffix: *travelling* /ˈtrævəlɪŋ/ becomes /ˈtræʌlɪŋ/. (Look back at p. 39 for similar cases with syllabic /l/.)

Notice also how the three syllables of *national* and *company* /ˈnæʃənəl/, /ˈkʌmpəni/ become two /ˈnæʃnəl/, /ˈkʌmpni/ and how the four syllables of *reasonable* /ˈriːzənəbəl/ become three /ˈriːznəbəl/, through the loss of the unstressed syllable before /n/. (In a similar way the four syllables of *comfortable* /ˈkʌmfətəbəl/ become three /ˈkʌmftəbəl/.)

The elimination of a weak syllable in a sequence of weak syllables also takes place across word boundaries, i.e. in phrases. Consider the phrase *matter of fact* /ˈmætər ə ˈfækt/; there is a sequence of two unstressed syllables separated by /r/ in a way that is exactly parallel in the case of lexical items like *mystery* and *interest*. What regularly happens is that the unstressed syllable before /r/ will disappear: /ˈmætr ə ˈfækt/. Consider these phrases and transcribe them in the same colloquial style

7.118   after a while   _____
        brother in law   _____
        mother and toddlers   _____
        doctor in the house   _____
        offer advice   _____

        and also

        travel at night   _____
        open at nine   _____

Finally, it is worth noting that some speakers eliminate an unstressed vowel at the beginning of certain words before /r, l/, as in *correct* /kəˈrɛkt/ becoming /ˈkrɛkt/ and *collect* /kəˈlɛkt/ becoming /ˈklɛkt/. Consider these words and transcribe them in this colloquial style

7.119   terrific   _____
        police   _____
        eleven   _____
        parade   _____
        verandah   _____

Notice how *perhaps* /pəˈhæps/ alternates with /pəˈræps/ and then also, more colloquially, with /ˈpræps/. And the verb *suppose* /səˈpəʊz/ is reduced to /ˈspəʊz/, especially in the phrase *suppose so*; a popular spelling, *s'pose so*, reflects this.

Similarly, in phrases with unstressed *for* and /r/ liaison, the neutral vowel before /r/ may disappear; for example, *for instance* may reduce to two syllables /ˈfr ɪnstənts/ from the three of /fər ˈɪnstənts/. Transcribe in this same colloquial style

7.120   for example   _____
        for everyone _____
        for £8   _____
        for a minute _____

We have now covered not only the processes of simplification (Chapter 6) but also all the effects of rhythm that affect the pronunciation of phrases in English, and you should now be able to transcribe whole texts in a typical colloquial style.

So this is now what you can try and do! There are three texts that follow. First of all, you could try to transcribe the story of Goldilocks in a typical, careful reading style, as if reading the story to a child. Guidance is given for each line.

Transcription text 1

7.121 *Goldilocks*

1 Once upon a time	epenthesis between /n/ and /s/. Weak form of *a*
2 there was a little girl	*there*: existential (weak) or locative (strong)? *was* is weak
3 called Goldilocks.	look for a case of elision
4 One day	both words are stressed
5 she went for a walk in the woods	Why is /t/ not elided? Notice /r/ liaison. What else happens to *for*?
6 all by herself.	*her* is unstressed, so loses /h/
7 And as she walked down one path	*And*: weak? What happens to the <s> of *as*? One case of elision, another of assimilation
8 she saw a nice house.	NB Intrusive /r/
9 Since she was full of curiosity	What happens to final /s/ of *since*? *Was* and *of* are weak
10 she walked close by	Do you notice another case of elision?
11 and noticed that the door	And yet another case of elision? Is *that* weak or strong?
12 was a little ajar.	Only one stress in this line
13 She knocked but there was no reply.	And yet another case of elision? Four weak words in this line
14 She called and there was still no reply.	Is the <ed> of *called* elided?
15 And because she was so curious	What happens to /n/ of *and*, /z/ of *because*? Is *so* weak or strong?
16 she decided to peep inside.	Why is the final /d/ of *decided* not elided?
17 There she saw a table	*There*: weak or strong? Intrusive /r/?
18 and on the table	Is *on* stressed on this occasion?
19 there were three bowls of porridge –	*There*: weak or strong? *Were* is weak
20 a big one, a middle-sized one, and a little one . . .	Note the compound word stress; and a case of elision?
21 Again because she was so curious	The /n/ of *again* does not assimilate because of the pause; but there *is* a case of assimilation elsewhere
22 she actually took a spoonful from the big one	Note the pronunciation of *actually*
23 but it was too hot.	*But*: weak or strong?
24 So she took a spoonful from the middle-sized one	*So*: weak or strong? *Spoonful* is a compound See line 20

25 but it was too cold.	First three words all weak
26 And then she took a spoonful	*Then* is stressed
27 from the little bowl	
28 and that was just right	*That*: weak or strong? *Just*: weak or strong? Any elision?
29 and she took another spoonful.	
30 Before she realized it	*Before* is stressed. Is the <ed> of *realized* elided?
31 she had eaten it all up.	What happens to *had* ? NB Syllabic /n/
32 She felt quite full	Why is /t/ not elided in *felt*?
33 and decided to sit in one of the easy chairs.	How is *the* pronounced in this line?
34 There was a big chair	*There*: weak or strong?
35 but it was too hard.	See line 25
36 There was a middle-sized chair	See line 20 again
37 but that was too soft.	*That*: weak or strong? Why?
38 And then there was a little chair	*Then* is stressed
39 and that felt just right.	See lines 37 and 32, and then 28
40 But she leaned right back	A case of elision? /t/ of *right* is [ʔ] here
41 and it collapsed.	How is -ed pronounced here?
42 As she picked herself up from the floor	See line 7, then 41, then 6
43 she noticed the stairs.	A case of elision?
44 And being a very curious little girl	What happens to *and* here?
45 she went up	*Up* is not a preposition here; it is stressed
46 and there she found three beds.	Is *there* weak or strong? And a case of elision?
47 A big one but it felt too hard	
48 a middle-sized one,	See line 20 again, if you really need to
49 but it felt too soft	
50 and a little one that suited her nicely	*her*: weak or strong?
51 and because she felt so comfortable	See line 15. *So*: weak or strong? Notice how *comfortable* is pronounced
52 she fell asleep.	
53 In the meantime,	
54 the three bears returned to their home	Elision?
55 and were surprised to find	Another case of elision? What happens to /d/ of *find*?
56 the front door wide open.	Is /t/ elided, in *front*? Is <en> in *open* pronounced as a syllabic /n/?
57 Father Bear was even more surprised	A case of assimilation. Is the <ed> of *surprised* elided in this case?
58 to find that somebody had taken	*That*: weak or strong?

59 a spoonful of his porridge.	*His*: is /h/ pronounced here?
60 'Someone's been eating my porridge', he called.	How is *'s* pronounced here? *Been* is weak
61 'And someone's been eating <u>my</u> porridge', said Mother Bear.	*My* is strong here; so don't forget the stress mark; *said* does not have a stress mark here, but assimilation?
62 'And someone's been eating <u>my</u> porridge	
63 and eaten it all up', said Baby Bear.	Assimilation?
64 'And someone's been sitting in my chair', said Father Bear.	Assimilation?
65 'And someone's been sitting in <u>my</u> chair', said Mother Bear.	See line 61
66 'And someone sat on my chair	Assimilation?
67 and broke it', cried Baby Bear.	Two cases of assimilation
68 'Well, who's been in our house,	How is *'s* pronounced here? *Our*: weak or full?
69 while we were all out?' they asked.	*while* has a stress here, possibly because it is followed by a series of weak syllables. NB 'linking /r/'. What happens in *asked*?
70 'I'm going to look upstairs', said Father Bear.	Is *going to* pronounced stressed? Note the stress pattern of *upstairs*
71 'Hey, someone's been lying on my bed', he called.	Assimilation. Is the /h/ of *he* pronounced?
72 'And someone's been lying on <u>my</u> bed', said Mother Bear.	See line 61 again, if you must
73 'And someone's been lying on <u>my</u> bed	
74 and she's still there,	*There*?
75 fast asleep', said Baby Bear.	
76 His voice woke her up.	What two things happen to *her* here?
77 She sat up in bed	Assimilation?
78 and frightened by the sight of the bears,	The <ed> of *frightened* is elided, but what happens as a result?
79 she jumped down,	Another case of elision
80 ran past them	The /n/ of *ran* is kept, but what happens to the /t/ of *past*?
81 down the stairs	*down* is a preposition here, but is stressed
82 out of the house,	*out* is stressed
83 back into the woods	*back* is stressed, but *into* is not
84 and all the way home.	*(See Key)*

*

And now try this conversational monologue in a fairly colloquial style, with less guidance.

Transcription text 2

7.122 *Travelling to Italy*

1 We've been to Italy a couple of times	Is *been* stressed here? Watch out for *to*, and *of*
2 We've driven both times	Watch out for a case of assimilation
3 I don't mind driving	Remember the problem of *n't* (and elision!)
4 I really quite enjoy it	
5 But in <u>those</u> days	*Those* takes a strong stress here
6 you had all different currencies	Remember the problem of *-nt*
7 We stayed overnight in Dunkirk	*Overnight* is a compound adverb here. Don't forget what happens to /n/ before /k/
8 and paid for bed and breakfast	Cases of assimilation
9 in French francs	/n/ before /k/ again
10 Then we drove to Belgium	
11 and paid for mid-morning coffee	How many cases of assimilation in this line? *Mid-morning* is a compound adverb turned adjective followed by a stressed word; get its stress right!
12 in Belgian francs	And in this?
13 and then on into Luxembourg	
14 We bought petrol there	Why is /t/ not elided? *There*: weak or strong?
15 because it was cheaper	Is *because* stressed or not?
16 and so we used their currency	Elision? *Their* takes a strong stress here
17 and we stopped for a picnic there too	Elision? What happens to *for*? *There*?
18 And then in the afternoon	NB *The* before a vowel. *Afternoon* is a compound, but which part has primary stress?
19 we drove on into Germany	NB *on* is not a preposition here
20 had some food	*Some*: weak or strong?
21 and of course	Remember what can happen to *of* in this phrase
22 we had to pay for that in marks	*Had*: weak or strong? And *that*? Assimilation?
23 Four different currencies by tea-time	
24 We stayed with a friend's family	Elision?
25 in Southern Germany	
26 And the following day	
27 crossed the border into Switzerland	Elision? Liaison?
28 And there of course we used Swiss francs	*There*: weak? Liaison? We would normally expect elision of /d/ in *used* in a case like this one, but the speaker appears to stumble, and does not elide.
29 Then over into Italy	Liaison? Look at line 1 again
30 where we had to start using	Work out what happens to /t/ + /j/ here

31 Italian lira

32 Six currencies in two days

33 We knew of course before we
started

before is not strong here

34 that we would need all this

Would: weak?

35 so we had bought a bit of each

Had: weak? And what else happens?

36 but on the way back

NB *on* is stressed here

37 we converted bit by bit

Assimilation?

38 all the currency that we wouldn't
need again

Work out the *n't* here

39 changing all our lira into Swiss
francs

Liaison?

40 and then all that into German
marks.

Assimilation?

41 Quite crazy

42 and we probably lost quite a
bit that way

Elision?

43 But now, they use euros all
the way

The /z/ of *use* is retained here, although it could
have easily become /ʒ/

44 except Switzerland

Elision?

45 it's so much easier

So: weak or strong?

46 and so you don't lose so much

So twice: weak or strong in each case?

*

(See Key)

And finally this conversational monologue with no guidance.

Transcription Text 3

7.123 *9/11*

we were actually in America at the time . uh we'll always remember the eleventh of September of course . we were staying with friends in San Francisco . we'd put our Jonathan . on a plane back to LA . uh . because he had to get . back for his classes . but we couldn't help but think then . at the time . how lax their idea of security was . you know he actually offered his coat to them and opened his bag and so on . but they just waved him through . as if he was . catching a bus . and I remember thinking then . that wouldn't happen in Britain . not even in Cardiff . you know just like . you know . our little airport like Cardiff . that was the . that was the Monday morning . and then on the . that was the Monday evening . then on the Tuesday morning . I got up . and went to make a cup of tea . you know . to get going in the morning . Karen our friend . was already up . and was about to go off jogging . when there was a phone call . and *as* she was talking on the phone . she switched the television on . and I thought that was strange . you don't normally turn the . TV on . when you're talking to somebody on the phone . well it was her husband Jim . *he'd* heard . of a disaster in New York on his way to work . not knowing quite what was happening . and

128

there on the screen . we saw one of the towers . blazing away . and there was a strong suspicion . that this was no accident . and then on the screen . came this second plane . looking as if it was heading deliberately . at the at the other tower . and there before my very eyes . the most appalling disaster was unfolding . I called Charlotte . my wife . to come and see . she'd still been in bed . waiting for that cup of tea . you've got to remember . that San Francisco's about . three hours behind New York . so when it was ten over in New York . it was only uh it was only seven where *we* were . so there we were . the three of us . watching this horrible disaster unfolding on TV . Charlotte and me and Karen . as I said Jim had gone off to work early that morning . well it was incredible . we were just stunned by it all . we just couldn't believe what we were watching . it was more of a horror film than reality . and then the first tower crumbled . this was . more than a bad movie . and then unbelievably the second tower as well . I still remember the horror . of watching it all happen *as* it happened . and the great . billowing of dust and smoke . pouring down the streets at a frightening speed . and then of course there was the Pentagon plane too . and the terrific devastation there too . there was a fourth hijacked plane . and we learned of the heroic efforts of the . passengers . knowing that they were going to die for a . for certain . but they seized the hijackers . and rammed the plane . into the ground . but off target . people assumed that it was heading towards Washington . we sat there . bewildered . stunned . overcome with the power of it all . so much to take in . all of it staggering . we sat there silent . open-mouthed . shocked . we remained quiet all morning . and then the first fatalities were being named . those planes . had been on their way to LA . and San Francisco . so the majority of the dead . were . local men and women . their names were appearing on a moving line at the bottom of the screen . practically all of them local people . it was just so dreadful . Karen had had the day off . but she decided to go into school later on . she's a school counsellor . and felt that she should be there to help . *we* left in the afternoon . I got petrol in their local garage . there was just this awful eerie silence among the people . it was as if the whole city had gone quiet . oh what a day *that* was

⋆

(See Key)

You have now completed one of the most thorough and comprehensive introductions to the transcription of rhythm in phrases in English that is available anywhere. There will not be an English phrase now that you will not be able to transcribe, in either an informal or a more formal style!

8 Intonation: tonality

Introduction

Spoken discourse not only uses rhythm as a resource, but intonation too. What is intonation? Intonation is the linguistic use of *pitch* in discourse. It is *linguistic*, in the sense that it carries meaning; changing the intonation of an utterance can easily change the meaning of that utterance. For instance, the clause

- you understand, don't you

has one meaning if the tag is accompanied by a falling tone, but a different meaning if it is accompanied by a rising tone. (Say it to yourself, to make sure!) The notion of *linguistic* can be extended to include the *paralinguistic* use of intonation, in which something of the mood or attitude of the speaker is conveyed, for instance whether the speaker is angry, bored, insistent, etc. *Linguistic* might also be extended to include *sociolinguistic* variation of the kind that shows where a person comes from; for instance, the intonation of working-class Bristolians is quite different from, say, that of middle-class Glaswegians. For practical purposes, in this workbook, we will have to focus on just the one variety, SESP.

Note also that we need to make the distinction between intonation and lexical tone in tone languages. In tone languages, a change of tone (i.e. pitch) may change the meaning of a word/lexical item, as in Cantonese:

8.1 si ˥ 'silk' (high level)
si ˧ 'to try' (mid level)
si ˨ 'matter' (low mid level)
si ˩ 'time' (low level)
si ˧˥ 'history' (mid to high rising)
si ˩˧ 'city' (low to mid rising)

but in a non-tone language like English, a word like *see* will keep its lexical meaning even when accompanied by different tones/pitches, but its meaning in discourse might change:

8.2 *see* ˥ said insistently
see ˧ said in a bored manner, as if to mean *I knew it would happen*
see ˨ said in a cold manner
see ˩ said in a cold manner
see ˧˥ said in a challenging manner, as if to mean *Do you understand now?*
see ˩˧ said in an appealing manner, as if to mean *I did tell you.*

Intonation in English is thus the *linguistic* use of pitch in *discourse*, but it comprises more than **tone**. When we talk, we usually have more to say than just one piece of information; sometimes it might only be one piece of information, like *Thank you*, but usually it is much more. Each piece of information is conveyed by a *unit of intonation*; these units of intonation – called, by others, *tone units*, *tone groups*, *intonation contours* or *intonation phrases* – constitute the **tonality** of spoken discourse. As we will soon see, changes in tonality also effect changes in meaning.

Thirdly, each intonation unit has a word which is more prominent than the others; they are made more prominent by a distinctive pitch movement or level and loudness. These words constitute the nucleus, or tonic, of the intonation unit and indicate the specific point of information, i.e. what the unit of intonation focuses on. These prominent, nuclear (tonic) words constitute the **tonicity** of spoken discourse; again, changes in tonicity effect changes in meaning.

Tonality, tonicity and tone are the basic systems that operate in English intonation; choices in all three systems are made every time we say something. We always use all three systems together, although we can vary them in order to create different meanings. Take the example of *You understand, don't you*. Listen to these three different renderings

8.3 you under\stand | \don t you
     you under\stand | /<u>don</u> t you
     \<u>you</u> understand | /<u>don</u> t you

The tonality of all three renderings consists of two units of intonation; the upright bar (|) marks unit boundaries.

The tonicity of the first two is the same, with the words *understand* and *don't* the most prominent in each of their units; <u>underlining</u> marks out the tonic *syllable* of each word. The tonicity is different in the first unit of intonation in the third rendering, where *you* was chosen as the prominent; this will only make sense if a contrast is being made with somebody else who presumably does *not* understand.

The tones in each unit vary between falling (\) and rising (/). In the first rendering, the tag *don't you* is accompanied by a falling tone, which suggests that the speaker thinks that they know they are right; but in the other two renderings, the tag is accompanied by a rising tone, which suggests that the speaker is not sure whether they are right or not.

You will be given guidance and practice in all three systems. We begin with the case of tonality, because most of our spoken discourse is longer than a single piece of information. We need to know the tonality of the discourse before we can investigate the tonicity of each unit of intonation; and we need to know the tonicity of the unit before we can safely identify the tone that has been chosen. This 'hierarchy' of systems is the basis of the way these final Chapters of the workbook are organized.

However, before we get into the programme, we need to identify the parts of an intonation unit, in order to show where the potential for intonational contrasts lies. Let us take the sentence *I wish I understood it*; a native speaker of English is most likely to say it as

8.4   I wish I under\stood it

as one single piece of information (i.e. as one intonation unit), with focus on *understood* and a falling tone to indicate a statement. The structure of the unit consists, at one level, of two parts:

1. the part that includes the tonic syllable with its distinctive tone, and any syllables that follow (in this case -\stood it); this is called the **tonic segment**;
2. all the rest of the intonation unit that precedes the tonic segment (in this case *I wish I under*-); this is called the **pretonic segment**.

The tonic segment is usually divided into two: the **tonic syllable** itself, and the remaining syllables, often called the **tail**. The pretonic segment is also usually divided into two: the segment that contains the first stressed syllable and all the remaining syllables up to the tonic syllable – this segment is often called the **head**; any unstressed syllables preceding the head are often called the **pre-head**. All four segments are illustrated in the example:

pretonic segment | tonic segment

I 'wish I under\stood it

pre-head | head | tonic | tail

There is the potential for contrasts not only in the tonic syllable but in the head and pre-head segments too; that is why we need to identify them. The tail does not usually carry contrasts, but it does carry pitch changes for the compound tones (see later).

The tonic syllable is obligatory; if a unit of intonation is begun, but no syllable is made tonic, then we conclude that that intonation unit has been abandoned. This sometimes happens in informal discourse, as a speaker changes their mind and starts an intonation unit afresh. The tail, head and pre-head are all optional, in the sense that they may perhaps not be required in the construction of an intonation unit. Consider these examples:

8.5   I 'wish I under\stood   (no tail)
       \think about it   (no head, no pre-head)
       I'll \think about it   (pre-head, but no head, since the first stressed syllable happens to be the tonic syllable)
       \think   (tonic syllable only; no head, no pre-head, no tail)

Symbols

The symbols used in this workbook are, in general, consistent with Crystal (1969, 1975), Tench (1996) and Wells (2006); see the panel below for the minor differences with Wells. These symbols are simple and economic to use; their design is relatively iconic, and are as follows:

| = intonation unit boundary
under<u>lin</u>ing = tonic syllable
' = non-tonic stressed syllable
\ = falling tone
/ = rising tone
v = falling-rising tone
∧ = rising-falling tone
– = level tone
- = pause (equivalent to a syllable)
. = brief pause
(xx) = indecipherable
(*laughter*) = relevant note

		Wells	Halliday	Brazil	ToBI
feature					
paratones	‖	‖		‖↑	
intonation units	|	|	//	//	%
tonic syllables	<u>tonic</u>	<u>tonic</u>	<u>ton</u>ic, **ton**ic	<u>TONic</u>	
falling tone	\<u>so</u>	\<u>so</u>	1	*p*	H*L L%
low	\<u>so</u>	\<u>so</u>	1–		L*L L%
high	\<u>so</u>	\<u>so</u>	1+		
rising-falling tone	∧<u>so</u>	∧<u>so</u>	5	*p+*	L H*L%
low	∧<u>so</u>		<u>5</u>		
rising tone	/<u>so</u>	/<u>so</u>	2, 3	*r+*	L*H H%
low	/<u>so</u>	/<u>so</u>			
high	/<u>so</u>	/<u>so</u>			H*H L%
raised	↑/<u>so</u>		–2		
mid level tone	–<u>so</u>	><u>so</u>		*o*	H*H L%
falling-rising tone	v<u>so</u>	v<u>so</u>	4, <u>2</u>	*r*	H*L H%
low	v<u>so</u>		<u>4</u>		
non-tonic stress	'<u>so</u>	'<u>so</u>	/	nonTONic	H, L
high head	<u>so</u>	'<u>so</u>		↑	H[1]
low head	_<u>so</u>	,<u>so</u>	–2, –3	↓	L
falling head	↓ <u>so</u>	\<u>so</u>			H+H*L%
rising head	↑ <u>so</u>	/<u>so</u>	–1		L+L*H%
pause	-		∧		
brief pause	.				

[1] i.e. an initial H or L in the 'intonational phrase' (see Gussenhoven 2004)

Other authors use different symbols. Pike (1945), for instance and those in his Tagmemic tradition used a set of numbers to indicate pitch heights. Halliday (1967, 1970; see also Halliday & Greaves 2008) use a set of numbers to indicate whole 'tunes'; Brazil (1975; 1997) and those in his Birmingham Discourse Intonation tradition use letters to indicate 'tunes', but both are relatively easily converted to the above; see the panel below. Pierrehumbert (1987), Ladd (1996), Beckman & Elam (1997), Gussenhoven (2004) and others use the Tone and Break Index, 'ToBI', and a set of letters and symbols to indicate pitch height and movement. It is difficult to 'translate' these ToBI formulae, because there does not seem to be an equivalent theory of information structure or a clear designation of tonicity; furthermore, there are differences between these four authors, but an attempt is made in the panel below to compare Gussenhoven's system with that introduced here. The ToBI approach is used widely in North America. (Gaps in the panel indicate that a particular feature is not recognized in that particular system.)

Tonality

Tonality is the division of spoken discourse into discrete units of intonation, each of which carries one piece of information. This function can easily be demonstrated by listening to one sentence spoken with different tonality:

8.6   i they're coming on \Monday
      ii they're \coming | on \Monday

The first rendering presents just one piece of information, whereas in the second, the speaker first tells one thing ('they're coming') and then adds a second piece of information (i.e. *when* they are coming). There is thus a contrast in tonality, and that contrast signals a different distribution of information. Tonality thus represents the way the speaker perceives all the information and then organizes it into units of intonation.

As often as not, tonality boundaries coincide with clause boundaries; and there is good reason for this. A clause is designed to convey reference to a situation or happening, with a verb indicating the activity or state of affairs, and nouns (and nominal groups) representing the participants; adverbs and prepositional phrases represent reference to any circumstances; conjunctions represent links between the situations or happenings. A clause, in essence, is the *grammatical* means of representing pieces of information – an activity or state of affairs, participants, circumstances and linkage. And an intonation unit, in essence, is the *phonological* means of representing pieces of information in spoken discourse. In this way, there is a neat congruence of phonology, grammar and semantics (the 'pieces of information'); when this congruence is actually realized in spoken language, we speak of **neutral tonality**: a single unit of intonation representing a single piece of information worded as a single clause. This was the case, for instance, in i above.

Neutral tonality accounts for at least half of the instances of intonation units in informal conversation. Listen to the following account of a dangerous childhood prank: listen for the intonation units and mark them with the upright bar (|), and then notice how often – but not always! – the tonality boundaries coincide with clause boundaries. Listen as often as you need; concentrate on lines 5 to 17, since the speaker is still sorting out the story in his mind in the earlier lines, 1 to 4.

8.7 *Dangerous childhood pranks* 1

A:	my cousin Mervin . that was in the REME . uh . got me a thirty eight	1
B:	gun	2
A:	Wesson . Smith and Wesson . special . and Benny's . no it wasn't	3
	it was Rick Holmans's shed . and Benny . Brian Beddingfields .	4
	knew his dad had some . ammunition . from the war . and he found	5
	it and they were thirty eight . so we um . took them over the	6
	marshes and shot a couple of rounds off and that was great and	7
	then one . one day we were in up Prospect Road . near the scout	8
	hut . in a shed . in a . um Rick Holmans's shed . so there was four	9
	of us in this . sort of eight by s . six shed – – and we were	10
	playing about with the thing . and we messed about with it and did	11
	the usu you know and and sort of said oh we'll put a cross in it	12
	and make a dum-dum of it . and fired it . in the shed . at . at at the	13
	bit of wood (*laughter*) . and this bullet went round the shed about	14
	three times . and we all just froze . (*laughter*) and this bullet went	15
	round and round and round (*laughter*) was absolutely outrageous .	16
	and we had no concept of what we what could have happened	17

You will, perhaps first of all, notice that the pauses do not always coincide with either clause boundaries or intonation unit boundaries; the reason is clear: pauses often indicate hesitation by the speaker in the process of composing their discourse. In line 5, for instance, the brief pause before *ammunition* seems to indicate the speaker's hesitation as he sought the right word, and not the division between one piece of information *knew his dad had some* and a second piece *ammunition*. But the pause after *ammunition* does seem to indicate the end of one piece of information and the beginning of a second piece (i.e. the *source* of the ammunition). The pause after *war* seems to conclude the whole clause *knew his dad had some ammunition from the war* and to prepare for the next piece of information *and he found it*. But there does not seem to be a pause between that piece of information and the next, *and they were thirty eight*. So although pauses may often indicate the boundary of intonation units, they are not absolutely necessary, and in any case, often indicate something quite different, hesitation.

Secondly, you will notice the movements of pitch throughout the discourse; for instance, there is a falling movement from a relatively high pitch on *-ition* and then on *war*, *found it* and *-eight*. These will turn out to be tonic syllables because they each appear in what seem to be separate intonation units. But the point here is that after each fall there is an eventual return to a higher pitch; the low end of the fall signals the end of one unit, and the beginning of a change of pitch is one of the signals for the next unit. Similarly, after a rising tone, there will be a return to a lower pitch.

Thirdly, there is a tendency for unstressed syllables at the beginning of an intonation unit to be articulated more quickly than those at the end; this may, however, be difficult to perceive or measure without instrumentation. Yet this change of pace also contributes to the impression that a boundary is being marked.

The clearest boundaries are marked by all three features: pausing, a change of pitch and a change of pace. Often, only two, or even only one feature is present. What also helps is the grammar; for example, *some ammunition* constitutes one single nominal group, and so it would be most likely that a piece of information will include the whole of it. Furthermore, as we have seen, clause boundaries are very likely places for intonation unit boundaries because they will also constitute pieces of information. Help also comes from a perception of the pieces of information as such – that is how we, the listeners, process the information. We processed the information of 8.6i as one piece, but we seem to hear two pieces of information in 8.6ii. Altogether, there is a whole set of phonetic, grammatical and semantic clues.

Now let us present that same discourse (from line 5) clause by clause, to see to what extent that there is a matching up of clauses and intonation units:

1.	knew his dad had some ammunition | from the war	5
2.	and he found it	5–6
3.	and they were thirty eight	6
4.	so we um took them over the marshes	6–7
5.	and shot a couple of rounds off	7
6.	and that was great	7
7.	and then one one day | we were up in Prospect Road | near the scout hut | in a shed | in a um Rick Holmans's shed|	7–9
8.	so there was four of us | in this sort of eight by six shed	9–10
9.	and we were playing about with the thing	10–11
10.	and we messed about with it	11
11.	and did the usu you know	11–12
12.	and and sort of said 'Oh we'll put a cross in it	12
13.	and make a dum-dum of it'	13
14.	and fired it | in the shed | at at at the bit of wood	13–14
15.	and this bullet went round the shed | about three times	14–15
16.	and we all just froze	15
17.	and this bullet went round | and round | and round	15–16
18.	was absolutely outrageous	16
19.	and we had no concept | of what we what could have happened	17

The matching up of clause and intonation unit – neutral tonality – is demonstrated in clauses 2, 3, 4, 5, 6, 9, 10, 11, 12, 13, 16, 18 – in at least twelve of the nineteen clauses. (In clause 11, there is only one main verb, *did*, because *you know* would be treated as a comment adjunct/adverbial (or discourse item); in clause 12, there is a reporting clause *said* with its complement *"Oh we'll put a cross in it. . .*, and thus only one main clause.)

But what about the others? When a clause and an intonation unit do not have common boundaries, the tonality is marked. **Marked tonality** was demonstrated in 8.6ii; usually, marked tonality is chosen when the speaker decides to present more than one piece of information within a single clause, as in that case. Occasionally, the reverse can happen when a speaker words a single unit of information/intonation as two clauses, for example:

8.8   he did I \saw him

Now let us examine the cases of marked tonality in the discourse.

   1.   knew his dad had some ammunition | from the war   5
The first unit contains the mental process *knew* and its complement, an embedded clause. It is potentially a 'candidate' for neutral tonality, but the clause has not yet been finished. The second unit has only a prepositional phrase – less than a clause; it provides additional information, like 8.6ii. Thus there is one main clause, but two units of information/intonation – marked tonality.

   7.   and then one one day | we were up in Prospect Road | near the scout
          hut | in a shed | in a um Rick Holmans's shed| 7–9
One clause, but five units of information/intonation – marked tonality. The first one is a case of marked theme; see below (p. 141). The other units present ever more detailed information about the location.

   8.   so there was four of us | in this sort of eight by six shed   9–10
One clause, but two units of information/intonation – marked tonality. The first presents existential information, the second the location.

   14.   and fired it | in the shed | at at at the bit of wood   13–14
One clause, but three units of information/intonation – marked tonality. The first tells us what happened, the second where it happened, and the third what the target was. The first unit is a potential 'candidate' for neutral tonality, but the speaker has decided to add further, separate, pieces of information in the form of prepositional phrases.

   15.   and this bullet went round the shed | about three times   14–15
One clause, but two units of information/intonation – marked tonality. The first tells us what happened, and the second its frequency. Again, the first unit is a potential 'candidate' for neutral tonality, since there is full complementation of the verb, but the speaker adds extra information in the form of an adjunct.

   17.   and this bullet went round | and round | and round   15–16
One clause, but three units of information/intonation – marked tonality. The first again tells us what happened, and the second and third the direction of the bullet, rather like a list.

19. and we had no concept | of what we what could have happened   17

One main clause, but two units of information/intonation – marked tonality. The first is a mental process, derived from *conceive*; the second is the complement of the process. The speaker appears to want to emphasize both the lack of conception *and* the possibility of a catastrophe – thus two pieces of information.

*

Now try a similar task, but this time with a discourse that was written to be spoken, as the script of a play. There is no 'original' audio recording as such, but simply the imagination of the playwright of how they expected it to be performed. But you too will be able to imagine how the dialogue could be spoken; but there might well be points where there is a legitimate choice – and you have the right to choose as if you were directing the play! Furthermore, in this extract from George Bernard Shaw's *Pygmalion* the three characters have very different accents, but the principles of tonality will apply to all of them.

Pygmalion, Act 2

HIGGINS	Why, this is the girl I jotted down last night. She's no use: Ive got all the records I want of the Lisson Grove lingo; and I'm not going to waste another cylinder on it. [*To the girl*] Be off with you: I don't want you.	1 2 3
THE FLOWER GIRL	Don't you be so saucy. You aint heard what I come for yet. [*To Mrs Pearce, who is waiting at the door for further instructions*] Did you tell him I come in a taxi?	4 5 6
MRS PEARCE	Nonsense, girl! What do you think a gentleman like Mr Higgins cares what you came in?	7 8
THE FLOWER GIRL	Oh, we are proud! He aint above giving lessons, not him: I heard him say so. Well, I aint come here to ask for any compliment; and if my money's not good enough I can go elsewhere.	9 10 11
HIGGINS	Good enough for what?	12
THE FLOWER GIRL	Good enough for yə-oo. Now you know, dont you? I'm coming to have lessons, I am. And to pay for em tə-oo: make no mistake.	13 14
HIGGINS	(*stupent*) Well!!! [*Recovering his breath with a gasp*] What do you expect me to say to you?	15 16
THE FLOWER GIRL	Well, if you was a gentleman, you might ask me to sit down, I think. Dont I tell you I'm bringing you business?	17 18
HIGGINS	Pickering: shall we ask this baggage to sit down, or shall we throw her out of the window?	19 20
THE FLOWER GIRL	[*running away in terror to the piano, where she turns at bay*] Ah-ah-oh-ow-ow-ow-oo! [*Wounded and whimpering*] I wont be called a baggage when Ive offered to pay like a lady.	21 22

The punctuation helps significantly as a guide to the tonality of this discourse, by indicating the boundaries of the clauses, which are usually short enough to contain single pieces of information and single intonation units. There may, however, be disagreements between two 'directors' of the play: one might imagine a slower pace of delivery than the other, in which case they might expect a greater number of units of information/intonation. Secondly, one might interpret the management, or distribution, of some information differently from the other – the 'legitimate choices' mentioned above.

The discourse also illustrates a number of other features of tonality.

- Exclamations are treated as pieces of information – little chunks of interpersonal information; for example, *Why* (line 1), *Nonsense* (7), *Oh* (9), *Well* (10, 15, 17) and *Ah-ah-oh-ow-ow-ow-oo!* (21).
- Restrictive (or defining) relative clauses are qualifiers within nominal groups and, as such, do not count as main clauses; they are part of the information of the nominal group to which they belong. Examples: *I jotted down last night* (line 1), *I want* (2).
- Mental and verbal processes often have a clause as their complement, with the whole structure comprising a single main clause. Examples: *You aint heard what I come for yet* (4), *Did you tell him I come in a taxi?* (5–6), *What do you think a gentleman like Mr Higgins* . . . (7–8), *you might ask me to sit down* (17), *Don't I tell you I'm bringing you business?* (18), *shall we ask this baggage to sit down* (19). All these cases would probably be spoken as single units of intonation.
- Long clauses of five stressed syllables or more (or even sometimes of only four or three) have to be broken up into manageable pieces: *Ive got 'all the 'records I 'want of the 'Lisson 'Grove 'lingo* (1–2) will probably get a break between *want* and *of the Lisson Grove lingo*, which is an interrupted qualification of *all the records*. Such breaks will come typically at syntactic boundaries.
- Clauses containing both a finite main verb and a non-finite verb constitute single clauses and single pieces of information. The non-finite verb may be part of a complement, for example: *I heard him say so* (9–10); *Ive offered to pay* (22).
- *I'm coming to have lessons* (13–14) seems to be a case of two clauses in one piece of information, since the first clause, *I'm coming*, contains no new information, rather like the first clause in 8.8 above. More on this in the next chapter on tonicity.
- Vocatives that occur at the beginning, or in the middle, of a clause usually have their own intonation unit, as a piece of interpersonal information; an example occurs in line 19. But vocatives that occur at the end of a clause may well be included within an intonation unit; an example occurs in line 7.
- Subject disjuncts at ends of clauses usually have their own intonation units, because of the significance of their interpersonal information. Examples: *He aint above giving lessons | not him* (9); *I'm coming to have lessons | I am* (13–14).

139

- Tags usually have their own intonation units, as separate pieces of interpersonal information. Example: *Now you know | don't you?* (13).
- Comment adjuncts at the end of clauses do not normally have their own intonation unit even if they superficially constitute a clause. Example: *I think* (17).

*

Each intonation unit carries one piece of information. When an intonation-information unit matches a single clause, tonality is said to be neutral. This typically happens when the clause is

- 'simple' – it has full complementation but nothing extra like adjuncts, tags, apposition, etc.
- 'straightforward' – it has its usual ('unmarked') structure
- 'short' – it has no more than five stressed syllables.

And in most informal conversation, each single clause is, in fact, simple, straightforward and short, as the above real and scripted examples of discourse illustrate.

There are, however, some regular cases of marked tonality.

'Marked' distribution of information. The most obvious regular case of marked tonality is where the speaker adds to the main message some information about the circumstances of a situation; for example

- *his dad had some ammunition | from the war;*
- *we were up Prospect Road | near the scout hut | in a shed.*

Listen to this exchange:

8.9   A: I haven't heard anything from Jake for a bit

8.10 B: But I saw him yesterday in the library

B's one-clause reply could be a single piece of information, spoken as a single intonation unit (= neutral tonality):

Bi   but I saw him yesterday in the library |

but he might have said it as two pieces of information:

Bii   but I saw him yesterday | in the library |

or even three:

Biii but I saw him | yesterday | in the library |

or even four, since a conjunction like *but* can have its 'meaning' of contrast highlighted:

Biv   but | I saw him | yesterday | in the library |

The renderings Bii to Biv are all examples of marked tonality, since the intonation unit boundaries do not coincide with the one clause. The speaker's marked distribution of information is the most obvious type of marked tonality.

Apposition is another regular case of marked tonality. Apposition refers to a second reference to an item within a clause as in, for example, *we were in a shed, in Rick Holmans's shed*, where there is a second reference to the same item *shed*. The phrase *in Rick Holmans's shed* is said to 'stand in apposition' to *in a shed*. It adds an extra piece of information and as such requires its own, additional, unit of intonation. Consider the following examples:

8.11　i　this is John | my neighbour
(*my neighbour* in apposition to *John*, adding an extra piece of information)
　　　ii　this is my neighbour | John
(*John* in apposition to *my neighbour*, adding an extra piece of information)
　　　iii　this is my neighbour | from across the road
(*from across the road* in apposition to *my neighbour* – extra information)
　　　iv　this is my neighbour | John | from across the road
(*John* and *from across the road* both stand in apposition to *my neighbour*)

An example occurred in ***Dangerous childhood pranks* 1**:

And Benny | . Brian Beddingfields　　　　　　　　　　　　　　　　4
(*Brian Beddingfields* in apposition to *Benny*, presumably as his real name).

Listing is a further example of regular marked tonality. Each item in a list constitutes an extra piece of information within a clause:

8.12　i　I'd like you to meet John | Joe | and Jack
　　　ii　all three are tall | dark | and handsome
　　　iii　they're all wearing smart suits | white shirts | and dark sunglasses
　　　iv　they are either neighbours | or friends |

Note, however, that coordinated items are not always treated as single items in a list: e.g. *black and white* could either be a list or a single item, as in *black and white shirts*; *shirt and tie* is often treated as a single item, as in *matching shirt and tie*.

　　　v　they never wear black and white shirts | nor matching shirt and tie |

Marked theme. When a clause element precedes the subject of a clause, the clause structure is 'marked'. The item that precedes the subject is referred to as the 'marked theme' and is placed there for informational prominence, usually to orientate the information of the clause to its context. Cases of marked theme are regularly given their own intonation unit in recognition of their informational prominence as, for example, in *then one day | we were up Prospect Road*. The marked theme may be an adjunct as in this case; *then one day* orientates the coming new information to what has just been said. Marked theme may also be the complement of a verb:

8.13　i　Joe | you wouldn't want to meet in a dark alley

Or a connective:

ii   however | Jack is very friendly
iii   whatever your problem | Jack'll help you
iv   if necessary | Jack'll lend you a bit of money

The marked theme may itself be a full clause like these examples from the *Pygmalion* extract:

- and if my money's not good enough | I can go elsewhere
- if you were a gentleman | you might ask me to sit down I think

or the main verb itself:

8.14   and go elsewhere | she did

Long clauses of five stressed syllables or more are regularly split into two or more intonation units at recognized syntactic boundaries – as we have seen in the two discourses examined above. Here is another example:

8.15   the 'train now ar'riving at 'platform 'three | is the e'leven 'twenty 'five | from 'Swansea to 'London 'Paddington

*

Now try another piece of real discourse. Mark the intonation units with | .

8.16   ***Dangerous childhood pranks* 2**

A:	the other thing that we used to do that Bernard mentioned when I was	1
	a little kid um . before um the sea front was all different it was just	2
	open . we used to . cycle down . especially on foggy days was the best .	3
	cycle straight down . Canute Road and straight off the prom into the	4
	sea – because we um . we d make sure the tide was sort of in . but you	5
	had to get rid of your bike in mid air	6
C:	but didn't you do that dreadful thing . to that boy	7
A:	o yeah	8
C:	where you were all kneeling down as (xx)	9
A:	it s about an eight or ten foot dive . in and you can dive at high tide	10
	. and Gus Hughes . came along one day . and we were always taking	11
	the mickey out of him . he s . you know he s one of these . the lads	12
	that . always got taken so we all . we all knelt down – with the water up	13
	to about there . he stood on the top and said . is it o k to dive we said	14
	yes – but of course it was only about knee deep – and he dived . and	15
	he stuck – and he just went crunch	16

You might have noticed in ***Dangerous childhood pranks* 2** at least a couple of cases where the speaker seems to start a piece of information but then decides to restart in a different way. In line 2, he hesitates after *a little kid* and starts the next piece of information with *before*, but abandons that beginning and starts again with *the sea front*. These hesitations, false starts and abandoned intonation units are all typical of real, unprepared, spoken discourse; but we still need to mark the beginning and end of each unit. An abandoned intonation unit will be identified as one without a tonic syllable, and this will become apparent in the next chapter, on tonicity. Another example of a re-start occurs in line 12: *he's you know*; the speaker then decides to proceed as before. You will also find a couple of similar cases at the beginning of ***Dangerous childhood pranks* 1**, but you are not likely to find such cases in the *Pygmalion* extract where the discourse is carefully worked out and then rehearsed by actors.

The speaker appears to 'stumble' intonationally in a couple of cases, which is, of course, typical also of real, unprepared, spoken discourse – in the same way as people hesitate over the selection of words, etc. In line 10, he seems to add *in* as a separate intonation unit after *it's about an eight or ten foot dive*. (With rehearsal, he would no doubt have done so.) He also seems to run *but of course*, which is in marked theme position, in line 15, into the rest of the clause, possibly because of the fast pace of delivery. If it was the script of a play, you might have directed him to slow down and treat this case of marked theme in the normal way, i.e. with its own intonation unit.

Tonality and grammatical contrasts

There are a number of cases where a change in tonality will signal a difference in grammar. Here is a simple example:

8.17   i this is my neighbour | John
       ii this is my neighbour John

As we have seen, i above will most likely be interpreted as a case of apposition, where *John* will be interpreted as a second reference to *my neighbour*. In ii *John* will probably be interpreted as a vocative; *John* is the person the speaker is actually addressing. In the written language, the two possibilities may well appear in identical form:

- This is my neighbour, John.

In this case, tonality has disambiguated an identical written form with the potential of two distinct clause structures.

Restrictive (defining) and non-restrictive (non-defining) relative clauses. A restrictive relative clause 'restricts' or 'defines' the reference to the particular case, as in *this is the girl I jotted down last night*; the relative clause, *I jotted down last night*, restricts the reference of *the girl*, in other words, defines which *girl* the speaker is referring to. But a non-restrictive or non-defining relative cause simply adds extra information which the speaker deems to be relevant to the discourse – hence also the term that is sometimes used, 'adding clause'. Here is an example of the two possibilities:

8.18   i the girl he jotted down last night | has come back
       ii the girl | who comes from Lisson Grove | has come back

The first, i, has a relative clause which defines which girl is being referred to (restrictive, defining); the second, ii, has a relative clause that is not meant to define, but to add relevant information (non-restrictive, non-defining), and because it is a clause that adds extra information, it is spoken as a separate unit of intonation. Now, of course, it would be perfectly possible to have two identically worded sentences with relative clauses that are either restrictive or non-restrictive, but it would be the tonality that, again, disambiguates the two grammatical categories:

iii the girl who comes from Lisson Grove | has come back

Which girl? The one from Lisson Grove, not the one from somewhere else! Now, compare these two instances:

8.19   i my brother who lives in Africa | is an economist
       ii my sister | who lives in Weston | is a care worker

How many brothers, and how many sisters does the speaker have? The tonality of the first, i, suggests a restrictive relative clause; so this suggests that the speaker has more than one brother and needs to define which one is being referred to. The tonality of ii suggests a non-restrictive relative clause; so this suggests only one sister, who is described further by where she lives. Again, compare these two possibilities:

8.20   i the girl who came in a taxi | wants some lessons
       ('Which girl?' 'The one who came in a taxi – not any other girl!')
       ii the girl | who came in a taxi | wants some lessons
       (We know already which girl. The extra information that she came in a taxi tells us something relevant – that she can probably afford the lessons!)

This difference can also be maintained in instances with less than a full relative clause. Compare:

8.21   i the girl wearing a hat with three ostrich feathers | came in
       ii the girl | wearing a hat with three ostrich feathers | came in

and

8.22   i the man with sunglasses | is Joe
       ii the man | with sunglasses | is Joe

A similar distinction can also be made in cases of apposition. Below, i defines which *Tom Jones* is being referred to, whereas ii does not:

8.23   i Tom Jones the singer | comes from the Valleys
       ii Tom Jones | the singer | comes from the Valleys
       In ***Dangerous childhood pranks* 1**, speaker A refers to his cousin Mervyn, identifying which of his cousins he means. With a tonality boundary between *cousin* and *Mervyn*, it would be understood that he only had one cousin, who he then decided to name.

144

Compare:

8.24 i my cousin Mervyn | got me a gun |

ii my cousin | Mervyn | got me a gun |

Notice he has only one cousin Mervyn, but he decides to add some relevant information through a non-restrictive (non-defining) relative clause, *that was in the REME*, which is spoken as a separate intonation unit.

In *Dangerous childhood pranks* **2**, speaker A begins with a restrictive relative clause, *that we used to do*, which is contained within the intonation unit that begins *the other thing*; and then he proceeds with a non-restrictive relative clause, *that Bernard mentioned*, which adds further, relevant, information which is accorded its own intonation unit. Also: *that always got taken* (line13), a restrictive relative clause that is contained within an intonation unit and defines which kind of lad that the boy was.

Apposition and complements. Some verbs can require more than one complement. This sets up the possibility of a sequence of nominal groups that can be interpreted as either a sequence of complements or a single complement and a case of apposition. Listen to these identically worded clauses:

8.25 i she considered Mr Higgins a gentleman | ('assessed as a gentleman'; *a gentleman* is a second complement)

ii she considered Mr Higgins | a gentleman | ('gave due thought to him, especially in view of his status'; *a gentleman* is in apposition to Mr Higgins)

and

8.26 i the girl called Mr Higgins a teacher (*a teacher* is a second complement; that is what she said of him)

ii the girl called Mr Higgins | a teacher (*a teacher* is in apposition; she called him, presumably because he was a teacher)

Complements, and intransitive verbs. Some verbs, like *wash*, can function either transitively (i.e. with complements) or intransitively (i.e. without a complement): *she washed her hair; she washed* (i.e. herself). Now compare these pairs:

8.27 i she washed and brushed her hair | (i.e. she washed her hair and brushed it – one event; *wash* is transitive; *her hair* is complement to both verbs)

ii she washed | and brushed her hair | (i.e. she washed herself and then brushed her hair – two events; *wash* is intransitive; *her hair* is complement only to *brush*)

and

8.28 i she dressed and fed the baby | (*dressed* is transitive; *the baby* is complement to both verbs)

ii she dressed | and fed the baby | (*dressed* is intransitive; *the baby* is complement only to *fed*)

also

8.29   i she looked and felt uncertain | (*uncertain* is complement to both verbs)
ii she looked | and felt uncertain | (*look* = 'glanced around' – intransitive; *uncertain* is complement only to *felt*)

and

8.30   i he forgot the visitor | (*forgot* is transitive; *the visitor* is complement)
ii he forgot | the visitor | (*forgot* is intransitive; *the visitor* a gloss on the subject, 'subject disjunct')

and

8.31   i he's trying to help the professor | (e.g. Pickering is helping Higgins)
ii he's trying to help | the professor | (e.g. Higgins is trying to help)

Manner and sentence adverbs. Some adverbs, e.g. *honestly*, may function sometimes as an adverb of manner and sometimes as a comment on the message:

8.32   i he spoke to her honestly | (*honestly* = manner)
ii he spoke to her | honestly | (*honestly* = 'I'm being honest when I tell you that he did speak to her, even though you may doubt it!')

and

8.33   i he doesn't talk to flower girls normally | (*normally* = 'in a normal manner')
ii he doesn't talk to flower girls | normally | (*normally* = 'it is not normal for him to talk to flower girls')

also

8.34   i she sings happily to herself | (*happily* = manner)
ii she sings | happily | to herself | (*happily* = 'I am happy to say')

The comment is treated as a separate piece of interpersonal information.

Negative domain. Tonality plays a dramatic effect in cases where the domain of negation may be ambiguous. The following written form may have two quite opposite meanings:

• He didn't agree because of the money.

Either the person refused because the money was not right; or he did agree, but it was not on account of the money. Listen to the two possibilities in spoken form:

8.35   i he didn't agree | because of the money |
ii he didn't agree because of the money |

In the first case, *n't* negates *agree*; in the second, *n't* negates *because of the money* (i.e. 'it was not because of the money that he agreed, but it was because of the challenge'). The domain of the negative is tied to the information within the intonation unit. Notice that in i above, the person did not agree, but in ii he did agree! (Examples like 8.35ii are very likely to have a falling-rising tone to indicate a point of contrast.)

8.36 i I didn't go | so that I could get promotion | (i.e. 'I got promotion by staying')
ii I didn't go so that I could get promotion | (i.e. 'I did go, but not with the intention of getting promotion'; with a falling-rising tone)

also

8.37 i he won't take notes | like last night | (i.e. 'he didn't take notes last night, and he won't now!')
ii he won't take notes like last night | (i.e. 'he took notes last night, but he won't do it in the same way now'; with a falling-rising tone)

Complex verbal groups and clauses of purpose. Sometimes a complex verbal group contains a second verb in the infinitive form, e.g. *come to hear* means 'happen, by chance, to hear'; and clauses of purpose often begin with the infinitive form of the verb, meaning 'in order to'. Consider the following pair: the first, i below, contains the complex verbal group and is therefore, basically, a single main clause, whereas ii below contains a clause of purpose as explanation of why *she came*. The written form might be identical, but intonation disambiguates conforming, in fact, to neutral tonality.

8.38 i she came to hear about the lessons |
ii she came | to hear about the lessons |

Similarly, *leave someone to do something* has the same potential ambiguity. Consider this next pair:

8.39 i she left him to think about it |
ii she left him | to think about it |

The first, i, has *leave someone to do something* as a complex group, meaning 'Higgins had to think about it'; the second, ii, has a clause of purpose, as an explanation why *she left him*, so that *she* could think about it!

A similar contrast can occur with reporting verbs with a complement that takes the form of an infinitive verb. Consider:

8.40 i tell him to settle the issue |
ii tell him | to settle the issue |

The first, i, has a report structure, with *to settle the issue* as the 'reported' complement: 'You must tell him that he must settle the issue.' The second, ii, has a clause of purpose: 'If you tell him rather than keep silent, that will settle the issue.' Also:

8.41 i shall we ask this baggage to save us the trouble | ('Please save us the trouble')
ii shall we ask this baggage | to save us the trouble | ('Shall we ask? She might go, and that would save us the trouble of throwing her out.')

*

Finally, mark the tonality boundaries in this (scripted) monologue.

8.42   ***Come on, Gus***

now then Gus don't be a fool like you were last time	1
next time check the tide seriously	2
the boys who tricked you will try again won't they	3
that was a dreadful thing they did pretending like that	4
I wouldn't trust them to be honest	5
my goodness me you could have injured yourself seriously	6
make sure they are standing up on their feet	7
tell them to be honest	8
call Bernard your friend well he wasn't much of one was he Gus	9
nor that other lad Joe	10
call Jack my friend to go with you next time	11
he'll deal with them frankly	12
he won't leave you to look after yourself he's too good a bloke frankly	13

*

Further information on tonality will be found in Halliday (1967, 1970), Tench (1996a, 1996b), Brazil (1997) and Wells (2006). Further exercises on tonality will be found in Beer (2005), Bradford (1988), Brazil (1994), Gilbert (1993: 'thought groups'), Hancock (2003) and Hewings (2004).

9 Intonation: tonicity

Tonicity is the location of the most prominent syllable in an intonation unit. Tonality represents the speaker's division of the total message into separate pieces of information; tonicity, on the other hand, identifies the focus of each piece of information. This function can easily be demonstrated by listening to one sentence spoken with different tonicity:

9.1 i they're coming on \Mon̲day |
    ii they're \com̲ing on Monday |

The first rendering focuses on *Monday*, whereas the second focuses on them *coming*. The second one can only make sense if some mention of the people's movements on Monday has already been mentioned or is already known, and now some contrast or correction is intended, e.g. they are not *leaving* on Monday! Tonicity tells you what the focus of the information is, whereas tonality tells you what the pieces of information are.

Each piece of information – each intonation unit – will have one focus, one tonic syllable. Occasionally, a speaker will begin an intonation unit but decide to abandon it before starting their information afresh; in such cases, there might be no tonic syllable and so we call such interrupted units 'abandoned' units: the full information was not given and the choices of focus and tone were not made either. Some examples were noticed in ***Dangerous childhood pranks 2***. Normally, however, each intonation unit will contain one tonic syllable; and the presence of the tonic syllable is obligatory for the delivery of a complete intonation unit.

What makes a syllable a tonic syllable? Usually, in each intonation unit there will be one syllable more prominent than the others; it is made more prominent by a degree of loudness greater than the other syllables, and it is accompanied by a distinctive pitch movement or level. There is sometimes a noticeable reduction in the pace of the syllables *after* the tonic syllable, compared to the quicker pace *beforehand*. All these clues help, but they may not always be present together. Try and identify the tonic syllables in these four sentences:

9.2 i   I think I'll go and have a cup of tea
    ii   where are you going on your holidays
    iii did you have a nice time
    iv look at that man up there

It should not be too difficult to identify them; they were the last words in the first three and the last one but two in the fourth sentence. Notice that they were all lexical items – content words, not grammatical items ('structural' words). In iv above, the last two words *up there* both belong to closed sets of locative adverbs and are thus treated as grammatical items. So, although *man* is not the last word, it is still the last lexical item. Note also that each sentence was a different clause type: a declarative, a *wh*-interrogative (i.e. non-polar), a *yes/no* interrogative (i.e. polar) and an imperative; the type of clause seems to have no bearing on either tonality or tonicity.

Neutral and marked tonicity

It is a general rule in English that the tonic syllable will be heard within the last lexical item of an intonation unit. This rule is pretty powerful, as in approximately 80 per cent of instances it will be found to be the case. This high proportion of tonic locations is known as **neutral tonicity.** Neutral tonicity refers to the phenomenon that the tonic syllable will occur within the final lexical item in its intonation unit. This is true for all examples above, apart from

they're \coming on Monday |

In the approximately 20 per cent of intonation units where this is not the case, tonicity is said to be 'marked'. **Marked tonicity** refers to those cases where the tonic occurs within a lexical item that is not final, like the example immediately above, or it occurs with a grammatical item, as in

9.3   they \are coming on Monday

Marked tonicity will always need a very particular context, as in these two cases. The second one, | *they \are coming on Monday* |, can only make sense in a context where the expectation of their arrival on Monday has been disputed or denied, i.e. the context is very particular.

New listen again to ***Dangerous childhood pranks* 1**. The tonality has already been investigated; we could transcribe it as below. But this time, listen for the tonic syllable in *each* intonation unit. Again, start from line 5, as the speaker was still sorting out the story in his mind in the earlier lines. Underline the speaker's choice of tonic syllable in each unit.

8.7 *Dangerous childhood pranks* 1

A:	my cousin Mervin | . that was in the REME | . uh . got me a thirty eight	1
B:	| gun |	2
A:	Wesson | . Smith and Wesson | . special | . and Benny's | . no it wasn't |	3
	it was Rick Holmans's shed | . and Benny | . Brian Beddingfields | .	4
	knew his dad had some . ammunition | . from the war | . and he found	5
	it | and they were thirty eight | . so we um . took them over the	6
	marshes | and shot a couple of rounds off | and that was great | and	7
	then one . | one day we were in up Prospect Road | . near the scout	8

hut | . in a shed | . in a . um Rick Holmans's shed | . so there was four   9
of us | in this . sort of eight by s . six shed | – – and we were   10
playing about with the thing | . and we messed about with it | and did   11
the usu you know | and and sort of said oh we'll put a cross in it | 12
and make a dum-dum of it | . and fired it | . in the shed | . at . at at the   13
bit of wood | (*laughter*) . and this bullet went round the shed | about   14
three times | . and we all just froze | . (*laughter*) and this bullet went   15
round | and round | and round | (*laughter*) was absolutely outrageous | 16
. and we had no concept | of what we what could have happened | 17

You might now notice how many of the tonic syllables occur with the final lexical item in each unit; these are cases of neutral tonicity.

Now try and identify the tonic syllables in the (scripted) monologue **Come on, Gus**. Again, the tonality of the monologue has been set out for you; all you have to do is underline the tonic syllable in *each* intonation unit. In line 1, there is one intonation unit that consists of only one word, *Gus*, and that word consists of only one syllable; in this case, there is no choice! Where there is more than one word in an intonation unit, there is a potential for choice; underline the choice that the speaker has made. Also, try and identify which syllable is the tonic syllable in a polysyllabic word, e.g. *holidays*. (We can distinguish, theoretically, between *tonic syllables* as a phonological feature, *tonic words* from a semantic perspective, and the grammatical distinction between *lexical* and *grammatical words* – note the interplay of all three 'levels of analysis'.)

Now underline what you think are the tonic syllables. There is no need to be concerned yet about the pitch movements you hear.

8.42 *Come on, Gus*

now then | Gus | don t be a fool | like you were last time | 1
next time | check the tide | seriously | 2
the boys who tricked you | will try again | won t they | 3
that was a dreadful thing they did | pretending like that | 4
I wouldn t trust them | to be honest | 5
my goodness me | you could have injured yourself seriously | 6
make sure they are standing up | on their feet | 7
tell them to be honest | 8
call Bernard your friend | well | he wasn't much of one | was he Gus | 9
nor that other lad | Joe | 10
call Jack | my friend | to go with you next time | 11
he ll deal with them frankly | 12
he won t leave you to look after yourself | he s too good a bloke | frankly | 13

Here are some hints:

Line 1: Which of the words *now then* is the more prominent? Is *time* more prominent than *last*, or vice versa?

Line 2: Which of the words *next time* is the more prominent? Which syllable is tonic in *seriously*?

Line 3: Which of the words *try again* is the more prominent?
Line 4: Can you think why *thing* is not prominent?
Line 7: Note that *up* is part of the lexical item *stand up*.
Line 10: Which of the words *other lad* is the more prominent?
Line 13: The tonicity of the first unit is tricky, so don't worry if you think there is more than one tonic syllable! Which of the words *good bloke* is the more prominent?

Broad and narrow focus

You will probably notice how often the tonic syllable occurs within the final lexical item of each intonation unit, but not always. It sometimes occurs on a non-final lexical item or on a grammatical item; we need now to investigate these cases of **marked tonicity**. Listen to these exchanges as extensions to the examples we introduced on p. 149; the tonicity of each first turn is marked by underlining, as discussed above.

9.4   A: I think I'll go and have a cup of <u>tea</u> |
      B: why don't you come and have a <u>meal</u> |

What A says could be the first turn of a new conversational exchange, and everything that A says would be new information to the addressee, B. But what B says contains a lot of information that A has given already: *you coming and having* refers exactly to what A said about *me going and having*. The only thing new in B's turn is *meal*; that is the focus of information in that unit. Because the focus is confined to just one element of the information, the focus is said to be **narrow focus**. This contrasts with the information of A's turn in which all the information was new; in a case like this, the focus is said to be **broad focus**. Broad focus refers to all the information in an intonation unit being new, whereas narrow focus refers to only part of the information being new.

9.5   A: where are you going on your <u>hol</u>idays |
      . . .
      B: where are you going on <u>your</u> holidays |

What A says above could be the beginning of a new topic in a conversation, which A and B proceeded with. Then later B might ask a similar question of A, but much of B's question is repetition of what A had said, except that *you* and *your* refer to A, not B! That is why *your* is the focus of B's question, a narrow focus, in contrast to the broad focus of A's original question. (Perhaps *you* might be tonic also, in which case B's turn becomes two intonation units with narrow focus in each: *where are <u>you</u> going* | *on <u>your</u> holidays* | .) The next example was:

9.6   A: did you have a nice <u>time</u> |
      B: we had an <u>awful</u> time |

What A says above, here, has broad focus, but what B says has narrow focus because the information *we having* (some kind of) *time* has already been given by A, i.e. A's *you* is the same as B's *we*. The last of those examples:

9.7　A:　look at that <u>man</u> up there

　　　B:　and look at <u>that</u> man | up <u>there</u>

What A says above, here, has broad focus; what B says has narrow focus. Even though B uses the same words as A, *that* and *there* contrast with A's message.

In all these cases, note that broad focus takes neutral tonicity – the tonic syllable within the final lexical item of an intonation unit. Narrow focus usually takes marked tonicity – the tonic syllable either within a non-final lexical item like B's response, *awful*, or within a grammatical item like B's responses, *your* (perhaps also *you*), *that* and *there*.

Occasionally, narrow focus has neutral tonicity like B's response with the tonic on *meal*. So, how do people distinguish neutral tonicity with broad focus from neutral tonicity with narrow focus? The answer is that information that has already been given is pitched low, whereas new information usually is not. Compare A's pitch on *I think I'll go and have a cup of* (the pretonic segment) with B's low pitch on *why don't you come and have a* (the pretonic segment). Thus we make a distinction between **new information** and **given** (or old) **information**.

Now you can see why, for instance, the speaker in ***Dangerous childhood pranks*** 1 line 9 has narrow focus on *Rick Holman's* and not upon *shed*, because *shed* is given information from the preceding intonation unit. The speaker in ***Come on, Gus*** lines 1 and 2 obviously regards *time* as given, referring to Gus's previous experience. In line 4, *thing* refers back to the previous experience also; hence, the narrow focus lies elsewhere (*dreadful* is the new information). In line 10, *lad* is given, showing that the speaker regards *Bernard* in a previous intonation unit as a *lad* also; so *other* is new, as narrow focus. Similarly, in line 13, *bloke* is treated as given information; the other people already mentioned are perceived as *blokes* too. The speaker also treats *he* in line 13 as new (narrow focus), although *he, Jack* has already been mentioned; he treats *he* as the focus as a way of contrast with the other 'blokes'.

Marked tonicity happens with numbers too. Perhaps most well known is the traditional tonicity of football scores read out on the radio. Compare these two scores:

9.8　i　Arsenal <u>nil</u> | Cardiff City <u>one</u> |

　　　ii　Arsenal <u>one</u> | Cardiff <u>Ci</u>ty one |

The first, i, has broad focus in both its intonation units as all the information they contain is new; tonicity is, therefore, neutral. (That was the score in 1927 for the only occasion when the English FA Cup went outside England!) The second, ii, represents a drawn game, with *one* common to the two units; *one* thus drops out of focus with the tonic syllable shifting to *Ci-*, which is marked tonicity. (NB In this instance, *one* is a lexical item as a number, and not a pronoun as in *he wasn't much of one.*)

Something similar happens in telephone numbers and the like

9.9　i　208 <u>7</u> | 424 <u>3</u> |

　　　ii　208 <u>7</u> | 42<u>3</u> 2 |

The first, i, has neutral tonicity, but in the second unit of the second, ii, the very final lexical item, *two*, is a repeat, and so the tonic syllable shifts to *thirt-*, creating marked tonicity.

Marked tonicity can also feature in parts of words like elements of compound words and affixes. Compare the word stress of these two instances of the compound *book case*:

9.10   i   we need a <u>book</u> case |

      ii   he's got a <u>book</u> shelf | but we need a book <u>case</u>

And then the word stress of these two instances of *disinterested*:

9.11   i   Jack acted in a dis<u>in</u>terested way |

      ii   <u>dis</u>interested | or <u>un</u>interested |

A kind of marked tonicity takes place when the final lexical item is a common verb of movement or happening which does not seem to add anything to the message; these are often called 'event clauses/sentences'. Listen to these:

9.12   i   the <u>phone</u> rang |

      ii   an <u>acc</u>ident has happened |

      iii   your <u>sis</u>ter's gone |

      iv   the <u>doc</u>tor's coming |

      v   an <u>am</u>bulance has been called |

The verbs are final lexical items, but they are semantically 'empty'. The 'movement' verbs do not add any information; it is the person who is moving that is significant. The 'happening' verbs are semantically redundant, because *ring* is what phones do, *happen* is what takes place with accidents, and in emergencies *being called* is what happens to ambulances. The verbs are required to fill syntactic places although they have little or no semantic effect. Technically, these verbs are lexical items in final position, but since they do not 'take' the tonic syllable, the tonicity is marked. (Because there is a kind of mismatch between semantics and syntax in these cases, linguists do differ in their interpretation of the phonology of the tonicity of these cases; I have presented a simple interpretation based on syntax.)

Final adjuncts

A regular case of marked tonicity happens when adjuncts which contain lexical items appear in final position in the clause, e.g.

9.13   i   where did you <u>go</u> last week |

      ii   what did you <u>do</u> all day |

      iii   there was nothing to <u>do</u> in town |

Adjuncts with no lexical content would not be expected to take the tonic syllable when they appear in final position, e.g.

154

9.14 i   what did you <u>do</u> today |
    ii   there's nothing to <u>do</u> here |

and it seems that adjuncts with lexical content follow suit. If they took the tonic syllable, they would sound very much as if the information had narrow focus. Listen for the sense of contrast:

9.15 i   where did you go last <u>week</u> | ('as opposed to just yesterday')
    ii   what did you do all <u>day</u> | ('not at night time')
    iii   there was nothing to do in <u>town</u> | ('as opposed to somewhere else')
    iv   what did you do to<u>day</u> | ('not yesterday')
    v   there's nothing to do <u>here</u> | ('as opposed to there')

Here are some more contrasting examples with final adjuncts:

9.16 i   he didn't want to jot it <u>down</u> again | (*jot down* = last lexical item; neutral tonicity)
    ii   he didn't want to jot it down a<u>gain</u> | (*again* = grammatical item; marked tonicity)

also

9.17 i   they needed to think it <u>over</u> together | (*think over* = last lexical item; neutral tonicity)
    ii   they needed to think it over to<u>gether</u> | (*together* = grammatical item; marked tonicity)

and

9.18 i   she might not come <u>back</u> then | (*come back* = last lexical item; neutral tonicity)
    ii   she might not come back <u>then</u> | (*then* = grammatical item; marked tonicity)

Final adjuncts which function for comment, viewpoint, reporting and glosses on the subject are usually 'out of focus', i.e. non-tonic, whether they contain lexical items or not. Here are some examples:

9.19 i   she wanted to speak like a <u>lady</u> though |
    ii   she wanted to speak like a <u>lady</u> of course |
    iii   she wanted to speak like a <u>lady</u> however |
    iv   she wanted to speak like a <u>lady</u> you see |
    v   she wanted to <u>speak</u> like a lady at least |

also

9.20 she was in a poor <u>state</u> economically | (viewpoint)

and

9.21 she wanted to have <u>lessons</u> she said | (reporting)

and

155

9.22 they re all the <u>same</u> these professors | (a gloss)

Certain adjuncts usually take the tonic because of the force of their meaning; thus they create utterances with marked tonality:

9.23 she wanted to <u>dress</u> like a lady | <u>too</u> | (also *also, as well*)

9.24 she wasn t sure about <u>Pickering</u> | <u>either</u> |

9.25 should she <u>leave</u> | or <u>stay</u> | in<u>stead</u> |

Finally, as we have already seen, vocatives in final position in the clause often are 'non-tonic' (look back at the second example in 8.17 on p. 143). This gives the potential for possible ambiguity with some verbs that can operate in either transitive or intransitive mode:

9.26 i   don t <u>shoot</u> Joe (*Joe* = vocative)
      ii don t shoot <u>Joe</u> (*shoot* = transitive; *Joe* = direct object!)

A similar ambiguity presents itself with reflexive pronouns acting as direct object and emphatic pronouns in final position:

9.27 i   she <u>asked</u> herself (*herself* = reflexive; 'she wondered')
      ii she asked her<u>self</u> (*herself* = emphatic: 'she was the one who did the asking')

*

Now try and identify the tonic syllables in

8.16 *Dangerous childhood pranks 2*

Once again, the tonality has been already investigated and can be transcribed as follows. Underline the tonic syllable in each intonation unit.

A: the other thing that we used to do | that Bernard mentioned | when I was	1
a little kid | um . before um | the sea front was all different | it was just	2
open . | we used to . cycle down | . especially on foggy days was the best | .	3
cycle straight down . Canute Road | and straight off the prom | into the sea |	4
– because we um | . we d make sure the tide was sort of in | . but you	5
had to get rid of your bike | in mid air |	6
C: but didn't you do that dreadful thing | . to that boy |	7
A: o yeah |	8
C: where you were all kneeling down | as (xx)	9
A: it s about an eight or ten foot dive | . in | and you can dive | at high tide |	10
. and Gus Hughes . came along one day | . and we were always taking	11
the mickey out of him | . he s . you know | he s one of these . the lads	12
that . always got taken | so we all . we all knelt down | – with the water up	13
to about there | . he stood on the top | and said . is it o k to dive | we said	14
yes | – but of course it was only about knee deep | – and he dived | . and	15
he stuck | – he just went crunch |	16

Hints:

Line 1: the very first unit is tricky, and you may hear two tonics, but which is the more prominent? More on this in the next chapter on Tone. Which is more prominent: *Bernard* or *mentioned*?

Line 2: treat | um . before um | as an abandoned unit.

Line 3: treat | we used to . cycle down | as an abandoned unit; the information seems to be abandoned before it is taken up again in Line 4.

Line 5: treat | because we um | as an abandoned unit.

Line 10: as we noted on p. 143, the speaker seems to stumble over the tonality of the first unit on this line; the tonicity must follow his tonality choice, which means that *in* will be the tonic syllable in its own intonation unit.

Line 13–14: *water* is the only lexical item in this unit, but does it take the tonic?

And finally, try and act the director again for this passage of **Pygmalion**, and underline the tonic syllables as you imagine them to be.

HIGGINS	Why | this is the girl I jotted down last night | She's no use | Ive got all	1
	the records I want | of the Lisson Grove lingo | and I'm not going to waste	2
	another cylinder on it | [*To the girl*] Be off with you | I don't want you |	3
THE FLOWER GIRL	Don't you be so saucy | You aint heard what I come for yet |	4
	[*To Mrs Pearce, who is waiting at the door for further instructions*] Did	5
	you tell him I come in a taxi |	6
MRS PEARCE	Nonsense girl | What do you think a gentleman like Mr Higgins	7
	cares | what you came in?	8
THE FLOWER GIRL	Oh, we are proud | He aint above giving lessons | not him | I heard	9
	him say so| Well | I aint come here to ask for any compliment | and if my	10
	money's not good enough | I can go elsewhere |	11
HIGGINS	Good enough for what |	12
THE FLOWER GIRL	Good enough for yə-oo | Now you know | dont you | I'm coming	13
	to have lessons | I am |And to pay for em tə-oo | make no mistake |	14
HIGGINS (*stupent*)	Well | [*Recovering his breath with a gasp*] What do you	15
	expect me to say to you |	16
THE FLOWER GIRL	Well | if you was a gentleman | you might ask me to sit down	17
	I think | Dont I tell you I'm bringing you business |	18
HIGGINS	Pickering | shall we ask this baggage to sit down | or shall we throw	19
	her out of the window |	20
THE FLOWER GIRL	[*running away in terror to the piano, where she turns at bay*]	
	Ah-ah-oh-ow-ow-ow-oo | [*Wounded and whimpering*] I wont be called a	21
	baggage | when Ive offered to pay |like a lady |	22

*

Further exercises can be found in Bradford (1988), O'Connor & Fletcher (1989), Bowen & Marks (1992), Taylor (1992), Gilbert (1993), Hewings (1993, 2004), Brazil (1994), Hancock (2003) and Cauldwell (2003).

10 Intonation: tone

Tone is the level and movement of pitch within an intonation unit. *Primary* tone refers to the system of contrasting movements of pitch within the tonic segment (i.e. tonic syllable and tail); the basic system is a choice between fall (\), rise (/) and fall-rise (∨). *Secondary* tone refers to variations to the basic primary system and also to levels and movements in the pretonic segment (i.e. pre-head and head).

The primary tone system functions in two dimensions: the speaker's organization of their information, and the speaker's role in interpersonal communication (whether the speaker is, for example, stating something, asking a question, telling someone to do something, greeting, wishing a happy birthday, etc.). The informational aspect of tone will be dealt with first, then the communicative aspect, in this chapter; secondary tones will be dealt with in the next chapter.

Tones

Listen to this statement:

10.1   we used to dive straight into the sea

You should hear it as one intonation unit with the final lexical item as the tonic. This means that the speaker intended this as a single *piece* of information (tonality) with broad *focus* (tonicity). The tone indicates the *status* of the information; in this case, it was a fall. The intonation of this example will now look like this:

10.2   we used to dive straight into the \sea |

with tonality, tonicity and tone all marked. Note that all three systems of tonality, tonicity and tone will always operate in every intonation unit – unless, of course, a unit is begun and then abandoned.

Now listen to the same wording with a different tone:

10.3   we used to dive straight into the sea |

The tonality and tonicity remain the same, but the tone changes to a rise, with the effect that the statement now sounds incomplete, as if the speaker is about to add something else (e.g. *but we got rid of our bikes in mid air*). The intonation of this second rendering will now look like this:

- we used to dive straight into the /sea |

The speaker thus has a choice between a fall and a rise (in linguistic terms, the speaker operates a system of tone). The rise in these cases 'means' **incomplete** information and depends on further information for it to make sense, whereas the fall 'means' that the information can be understood independently of any other information and can be considered as **major** information. It is the speaker who decides. The speaker knows what information they wish to provide and the status of each piece of information is indicated by their choice of tone. Listen to this statement:

we used to dive straight into the /sea | but we got rid of our bikes in mid \air |

The speaker uses the rise in the first unit of intonation to indicate that they have not completed the message, and uses the fall in the second to indicate that that was the main point of the message, the major piece of information. This sequence of rise + fall is inevitably a frequent feature of spoken discourse. Sequences of fall + fall are also very frequent:

10.4   we used to dive straight into the \sea | and get rid of our bikes in mid \air |

In this case, the speaker manages the message as two pieces of major information; that is how they viewed it on that particular occasion. Listen once again to ***Dangerous childhood pranks*** 1 and notice how many pieces of information are accompanied by falls. Mark each fall with \ directly before the tonic syllable itself. The tonality and tonicity have already been transcribed.

8.7   *Dangerous childhood pranks* 1

A:	| my cousin <u>Mer</u>vin | . that was in the <u>REME</u> | . uh . got me a thirty <u>eight</u>	1
B:	| <u>gun</u> |	2
A:	<u>Wes</u>son | . Smith and <u>Wes</u>son | . <u>spe</u>cial | . and <u>Ben</u>ny's | . no it <u>wasn</u> t |	3
	it was Rick <u>Hol</u>mans's shed | . and <u>Ben</u>ny | . Brian <u>Bed</u>dingfields | .	4
	knew his dad had some . ammu<u>ni</u>tion | . from the <u>war</u> | . and he <u>found</u>	5
	it | and they were thirty <u>eight</u> | . so we um . took them over the	6
	<u>marshe</u>s | and shot a couple of <u>rounds</u> off | and that was <u>great</u> | and	7
	then one . | one day we were in up Prospect <u>Road</u> | . near the <u>scout</u>	8
	hut | . in a <u>shed</u> | . in a . um Rick <u>Hol</u>mans's shed | . so there was <u>four</u>	9
	of us | in this . sort of eight by s . six <u>shed</u> | – and we were	10
	playing about with the <u>thing</u> | . and we messed a<u>bout</u> with it | and did	11
	the <u>usu</u> you know | and and sort of said oh we'll put a <u>cross</u> in it |	12
	and make a <u>dum</u>-dum of it | . and <u>fired</u> it | . in the <u>shed</u> | . at . at at the	13
	bit of <u>wood</u> | (*laughter*) . and this bullet went round the <u>shed</u> | about	14
	three <u>times</u> | . and we all just <u>froze</u> | . (*laughter*) and this bullet went	15
	<u>round</u> | and <u>round</u> | and <u>round</u> | (*laughter*) was absolutely out<u>rage</u>ous |	16
	. and we had no <u>concept</u> | of what we what could have <u>happened</u> |	17

In the telling of this narrative, the speaker handles practically all the new pieces of information as major; you can tell that he is 'composing' as he goes along, and the rapid sequence of falls probably adds to the sense of excitement he feels. There was at least one instance of rise + fall of some kind in lines 10–11:

- – and we were playing about with the /thing | . and we messed a\bout with it |

indicating incomplete information and then major.

The falls and rises are contrasting pitch movements on the tonic syllable; if there is a tail, it will end low with a fall, but high with a rise. That is an important clue if you feel unsure about the pitch movement itself. Listen to the pitch movement of these tones in tonic segments that contain tails:

10.5   i   we used to dive straight into the \reservoir |
       ii we used to dive straight into the /reservoir | . . .

In order to effect a fall, the pitch of the voice must start relatively high and then fall to a lower pitch, which is heard easily when there is a tail. But the relatively high starting pitch for the fall might be higher than the pitch in the pretonic segment, and it might sound to you as if the pitch has gone up before it goes down. This is one reason for identifying the tonic syllable clearly, in order to distinguish the pitch movement on the tonic syllable from the preceding pitch movement or level in the pretonic. It is the *pitch movement in the tonic segment that counts*, not any 'jump up' in pitch from the pretonic to the tonic; that 'jump up' is merely an adjustment to the pitch to reach the required level for the fall and is automatic (and, therefore, can never be contrastive).

Similarly, in order to effect a rise, the pitch of the voice must start relatively low and then rise to a higher pitch, which, again, is heard easily when there is a tail. But the relatively low starting pitch for the rise might be lower than the pitch in the pretonic segment, and it might sound to you as if the pitch has gone down before it goes up. This 'jump down' is the same kind of automatic adjustment that has just been mentioned for the fall. Again, it is the *pitch movement in the tonic segment that counts*. It is necessary to distinguish this automatic adjustment from the actual tone itself in the tonic segment. Here are those two examples again in 'slow motion'; notice the pitch adjustment between *the* (at the end of the pretonic) and *res-* (at the beginning of the tonic segment):

10.6   i   we used to dive straight into the \reservoir |
       ii we used to dive straight into the /reservoir | . . .

Another frequent sequence – beside fall + fall, and rise + fall – is fall + rise. Listen to this statement:

10.7   we used to dive straight into the <u>sea</u> | at high <u>tide</u> |

The tonality has been transcribed for you: two intonation units, two pieces of information. The tonicity has also been transcribed, as broad focus. The fall in the first unit indicates that the speaker is treating that information as major, but what does the rise in the second mean? It cannot mean incomplete information because of its position at the end of the sequence. In cases like these, a distinction is made between **major** and **minor** information; the final rise 'means' that this information is added as relevant, but it is treated as of only secondary importance compared to the major information. It has a lower **status of information**. Rises in this informational aspect of intonation indicate that the information has to be understood in relation to some other information; it has a status of being 'dependent' on something that the speaker treats as major ('independent').

Here are two other examples of fall + rise, i.e. of major + minor information, from ***Come on, Gus***, lines 5 and 13:

10.8   I wouldn t <u>trust</u> them | to be <u>honest</u> |

10.9   he s too <u>good</u> a bloke | <u>frankly</u> |

To be honest and *frankly* are added by the speaker as pieces of extra (interpersonal) information, rather like a comment, and are obviously going to be treated as minor. These last three examples would be transcribed as follows:

- we used to dive straight into the \<u>sea</u> | at high /<u>tide</u> |
- I wouldn t \<u>trust</u> them | to be /<u>honest</u>
- he s too \<u>good</u> a bloke | /<u>frankly</u> |

Minor information very often consists of final adjuncts. We saw in the previous chapter that they usually do not take the tonic unless they indicate a contrast, but they can appear in their 'own' intonation unit if the speaker wishes to give them some degree of prominence without making them the major information (like contrast). Listen to these statements:

10.10   I took a day off | last week
but there was nothing to do | in town
so I slept | the rest of the day

Other examples were also presented in the previous chapter; here are examples from p. 155 with final adjuncts given some (minor) prominence:

10.11   i   she wanted to speak like a \<u>lady</u> | /<u>though</u> |
ii   she wanted to speak like a \<u>lady</u> | of /<u>course</u> |
iii   she wanted to speak like a \<u>lady</u> | how/<u>ever</u> |
iv   she wanted to speak like a \<u>lady</u> | you /<u>see</u> |
v   she wanted to \<u>speak</u> like a lady | at /<u>least</u> |

10.12   she was in a poor \<u>state</u> | eco/<u>nom</u>ically |

10.13   she wanted to have \<u>lessons</u> | she /<u>said</u> |

10.14   they re all the \<u>same</u> | these pro/<u>fessors</u> |

Final adjuncts may therefore be treated as either major information (with \), or as minor information (with /) or as given information (non-tonic). It is the speaker who decides. They choose the information status that is required as appropriate to their purposes.

161

The system for information status so far is:

major   \
incomplete   / (non-final)
minor   / (final)

The complete system for information status also includes the fall-rise tone (∨). The fall-rise indicates major information that is somehow not complete in itself; it implies an extra, unspoken, message that the speaker expects the addressee to understand. The dimension of major information is indicated by the fall element; the incompleteness of the spoken message is indicated by the rise element. Listen to these examples.

Imagine Jack and Jill going out together for the first time, and then Jack's friends quizzing him about Jill, and Jill's friends quizzing her about Jack. They might ask him 'What is she like?' and he might reply:

10.15   \yes | she s o \k |

with positive major information, but if he replies:

10.16   she s o ∨k |

there is still major information, but it does not sound so positive because he implies another unspoken message which has a *but* about it. He does not deny that *she's OK*, but it is clear that there is another message which he expects his addressee(s) to be able to interpret too. This is **implied information**.

Similarly, Jill's friends might ask 'What is he like?' and she might reply:

10.17   he s very \nice |

with positive major information, but if she replies:

10.18   he s very ∨nice |

it does not sound as if she will plan to go out with him again! Her fall-rise also implies an unspoken '*but* message'. The major information is given; it is not denied, but its significance is compromised by an implied extra message. The extra message might not always be a '*but* message'; it might signal simply 'think about what this means' or 'this is my opinion on the matter'; for instance

• they re coming on ∨Monday |

might mean 'So we'd better get things ready for them right now'. The extra, unspoken, message that is implied is meant to be understood by the addressee from the connection between the spoken message and the situational factors.

Both the fall and rise elements are pronounced within the tonic syllable. If there is a tail, the two elements are spread though the tonic segment, e.g.

10.19   he s very con∨siderate

with the fall occurring on the tonic syllable and the rise delayed till the end of the segment, -*rate*. The ∨ symbol is placed just before the tonic syllable, since the placement of the rise element is automatic. (If you separate the two parts of the symbol as

- con\side/rate

it is possible that it might be interpreted as fall + rise, especially if there are a number of words in the tail.)

The fall-rise also occurs in a non-final position, and typically with the theme at the beginning of a clause. Its function then is to **highlight the theme**. An example occurs in *Come on, Gus* line 2:

10.20 ꮩnext time | check the \tide |

In this case, there is marked theme as something other than the subject appears at the beginning of the clause. Marked theme, as such, does not require to be highlighted with ꮩ, but the speaker chose to do so on that occasion. He could also have said:

10.21 /next time | check the \tide |

with a simple rise to indicate incomplete information; that would have been quite acceptable. But the speaker actually chose the fall-rise with the intention of drawing attention to the theme. A neutral theme could also be highlighted:

10.22 ꮩBernard | was not much of a \friend |

Theme is a notion about the information structure of the clause. We can now add the functions of the fall-rise in final and non-final positions to the system network for information status:

major information	\
minor information	/ (final)
incomplete information	/ (non-final)
implied information	ꮩ(final)
highlighted theme	ꮩ(non-final)

The system can be illustrated as follows:

10.23 Gus never checked the \tide |
Gus never checked the \tide | be/forehand
Gus never checked the /tide | . . .
Gus never checked the ꮩtide |
ꮩGus | never checked the \tide |

It should also be noted that the fall-rise can occur with questions and commands:

did Gus ever check the ꮩtide |
\Gus | check the ꮩtide |

The implication in the question is that the speaker is identifying the actual focus of the question: 'I think he might have checked other things, but I don't know about the tide' – a narrow focus with neutral tonicity. The implication in the command is similar: 'I think you should at least do that.'

It should also be noted that a change in the tone system is taking place in UK at present, by which the fall-rise is often used simply to mark incomplete information in non-final position in casual, informal discourse like **Dangerous childhood pranks 1**. this is probably how best to interpret the fall-rise in line 11:

- . and we messed a∨<u>bout</u> with it |

There does not seem to be a sense of an extra implied message here, and in any case, it is not final.

A final note on long tails! The longer the tail, the easier it is to decide whether the tone was a fall, a rise or a fall-rise. Take, for instance, line 1 of **Dangerous childhood pranks 2**:

the \<u>oth</u>er thing that we used to do |

The tail –*er thing we used to do* is kept on a low pitch throughout, which provides the evidence that the speaker had used a fall on the tonic syllable *oth-*. We could render that same statement as incomplete information:

10.24   the /<u>oth</u>er thing that we used to do |

with the tail rising slightly to a mid pitch; or even as highlighted them:

10.25   the ∨<u>oth</u>er thing that we used to do |

with the fall on the tonic syllable *oth-*, a low pitch through the tail until the rise element on the last stressed syllable *do*. If there is no stressed syllable in the tail, the rise element will automatically accompany the final unstressed syllable, as in 10.20 above. One final example must suffice: line 13 of **Come on, Gus**:

- ∨<u>he</u> won t leave you to look after yourself |

with the fall on the tonic syllable *he*, a low pitch through the tail until the rise element starting on the last stressed syllable *aft-* and continuing with the remaining unstressed syllables. The fall-rise spreads, or is 'split', throughout the tail, with the rise element automatically accompanying the final stressed syllable, or otherwise the final unstressed syllable.

We have now not only completed the study of primary tones in information structure, but also the study of all the intonation systems – tonality, tonicity and tone – in information structure. Choices in all three systems must be made for each intonation unit (unless it gets abandoned). The speaker decides how to divide their whole message into separate pieces of information, what the focus of each piece of information should be and what status each piece should have. But language does more than convey messages (the experiential metafunction); it also expresses speakers' communicative functions (the interpersonal metafunction), and it is to this that we now turn our attention.

Statements and questions

We have illustrated so far the use of tones in statements, whether those statements contained major, minor, incomplete or implied information or a highlighted theme. But people ask questions too, and tell other people what to do, and greet one another, and wish someone a happy birthday, and engage in many, many other types of communication.

A statement with major information takes a fall. Notice that we have combined reference to two metafunctions in that preceding sentence: experiential (major *information*) and interpersonal (*statement*). A statement means that the speaker knows some information and tells it to someone else. A question, on the other hand, means that the speaker does not know something and asks for that information from someone else who they assume does know the information. When the flower girl spoke to Mrs Pearce, she did not know whether Mrs Pearce had told Professor Higgins that she had come in a taxi; so she asks a question:

- Did you tell him I come in a taxi |

As the director of the play, you would expect her to use a rising tone as a signal that this was a question.

So rises indicate questions as well as incomplete and minor information. How can a person tell what function a rise carries in any given unit of intonation? The answer is not too difficult (at least, in theory!): if the rise is contained in an intonation unit that is attached to (or, 'dependent' on) another intonation unit that contains a fall (major information) or a fall-rise (implied information), then it indicates either incomplete information (if non-final) or minor information (if final). But if the rise is contained in an intonation unit that is independent, then it indicates a question. Compare:

10.26   i   this is the girl I jotted down last \night (he knows, and tells)
      ii   is this the girl I jotted down last /night (he does not know, and asks)

The tone contrast is parallel to the contrasting tones in tags, as we saw on p. 131

- you under\stand | \don t you
- you under\stand | /don t you

The first sounds more like a statement: a checking tag with a sense of being sure. The second sounds more like a question: a checking tag with a sense of not being sure and having to ask.

Questions like *is this the girl I jotted down last night?* are known as polar interrogatives, because the required answer is either *Yes* or *No* – hence the more familiar designation **yes/no questions**. They are usually accompanied by a rise:

10.27   is the tide /in
       is it deep e/nough
       shall I dive /in
       is it o /k

There is another type of question, the non-polar interrogatives which cannot be answered with either *Yes* or *No*. These questions usually begin with a *wh* item: *who, whose, what, which, when, where, why* and *how* – hence the more familiar designation **wh- questions**. They require the supply of some information. *Wh- questions* are usually accompanied by a fall. You might wonder why this is so, if the speaker is actually asking a question. The reason is that the speaker does, in fact, know the basic proposition of the message, but there is a gap that affects full knowledge. For instance:

10.28   who is in the water (they know that someone is in the water, but not who)
how deep is it (they know that it has some degree of depth, but not how much)
when is the tide right in (they know that the tide will be right in, but not when)
why are you kneeling down (they know that the others are kneeling down, but not why)
where have you put my bike (they know that their bike has been put somewhere, but not exactly where)

The proposition of the message might seem very simple as in

10.29   who are you (you must be someone, but I don't know who)
what is your name (you must have a name, but I don't know it)
how are you (you must be in some condition, but I don't know what)
why are you here (you are here, but I don't know why)

or

where are you (you must be somewhere, but I don't know exactly where)

Because the main proposition is known, even these short *wh-* questions will typically take a fall.
Commands also take falls. So, for instance when Professor Higgins tells the flower girl to go, he would almost certainly use a fall:

10.30   be \off with you

And when she replies with her protest, in an imperative clause structure, she too will use a fall:

10.31   don t you be so \saucy

Exclamations are also usually accompanied by a fall. These examples all come from the *Pygmalion* passage:

10.32   why (line 1)
nonsense girl
oh | we are proud
well (lines 10, 15, 17)

The use of primary tones for communicative functions described so far can be summarized as follows:

Statements: declarative clauses: \
Questions: polar interrogative clauses ('yes/no'): /
                  non-polar interrogative clauses ('wh'): \
Commands: imperative clauses: \
Exclamations: minor clauses: \

And this is as far as most traditional descriptions of English go. But our talk
– and life itself! – embraces much more than these five types of communication. The above summary is based on clause types alone, not upon the kind of
discourses that we engage in. We will now proceed with a fuller range of communicative functions in discourse, and for convenience will divide the range
into three general categories:

- knowledge, i.e. ways of sharing information
- influence, i.e. ways of influencing other people's actions
- social interaction, i.e. ways of relating to other people

*

Communicative functions which involve knowledge include statements and
the two kinds of question, but they also involve responses, agreement and disagreement, denials, affirmations, hypotheses, contradictions, conditions, etc.,
etc. In general terms, if the speaker knows something and imparts that information, they use a fall; if the speaker does not know something and seeks that
information, they use a rise. Put differently, the fall indicates *dominance* in the
communicative act (a person knows and tells), and the rise *deference* (a person
does not know; i.e. the person defers to the person who, they assume, does have
the knowledge).

    Statements take a fall and are usually worded as declarative clauses. But it is
possible to use a declarative clause for a different purpose with a rise:

10.33   he got you a /<u>gun</u> |

This is a **challenge**, with the intention of seeking confirmation that *he got
him a gun* is actually true. **Contradictions** also take a declarative clause with a
rise:

10.34   it wasn t /<u>so</u> dangerous

Wh- questions usually take a fall, but can also be accompanied by a rise for a
different communicative effect:

10.35   /<u>what</u> did he get you

This is an 'echo question'; it 'echoes' the wording of the previous speaker as a
way of seeking confirmation that they have heard correctly.

    Yes/no questions usually take a rise and are worded as polar interroga-
tives. But it is possible to use a polar interrogative with a fall, with a different
communicative effect:

10.36   aren t you going to dive \in

This is not so much a real question, but a statement that in the speaker's opinion the addressee should comply. This so-called **statement question** has also often been called a 'conducive' question, because the speaker is seeking to 'conduce' the addressee's response. Compare these two renderings:

10.37   i   were you /always taking the mickey out of him | ('I don't know; tell me')
         ii   were you \always taking the mickey out of him | ('I think you were')

Exclamations in interrogative form take a fall. Compare:

10.38   i   wasn t it /stupid | ('I don't know; tell me')
         ii   wasn t it \stupid | (exclamation like 'How stupid!')

We sometimes use polar interrogatives to get people to say something ('**prompts**') or as a preliminary to something we wish to tell ('**lead-ins**'):

10.39   have you considered the \consequences | ('Tell me what you think')

10.40   did you hear what happened to Gus \Hughes | ('Well, I'm going to tell you!')

Repeat *Yes/no* **questions** take a fall, as if the message is 'What I said was. . .':

10.41   A: did you get rid of your bike in mid /air | (genuine question)
         B: /pardon
         A: did you get rid of your bike in mid \air | (repeat question: 'What I said was . . .')

Similarly, **second attempt questions** take a fall:

10.42   A: was it ten foot /deep | (first question)
         B: \no |
         A: was it \eight foot then | ('second attempt' question)

Notice the difference between **closed list questions** and **open list questions**:

10.43   i   was it /you | or /Bernard | or /Joe | (open list question, not completed)
         ii   was it /you | or /Bernard | or \Joe | (closed list question; 'It was one of you')

and

10.44   i   did you take the /mickey out of him | or \not | (closed list question)
         ii   did you take the /mickey out of him | or was he just a \fool | (closed list question)

Responses usually take a fall, as do expressions of agreement and disagreement, etc.

10.45   \yes |
         \no |
         I don t \know |
         I \don t | \no |

that s \underline{\right} |

I disa\underline{gree} |

I don t sup\underline{pose} so !

not a\underline{t all} |

that s \underline{fine} with me |

of \underline{course} not |

Now try and identify the tones of ***Dangerous childhood pranks* 2**. Listen out for a few more rises than in ***Dangerous childhood pranks* 1**; they indicate incomplete or minor information or a question – but not all interrogative clauses are questions!

8.16 *Dangerous childhood pranks* 2

A:	the <u>oth</u>er thing that we used to do	that <u>Bern</u>ard mentioned	when I was	1
	a little <u>kid</u>	um . before um	the sea front was all <u>different</u>	it was just	2
	<u>op</u>en .	we used to . cycle down	. especially on foggy <u>days</u> was the best	.	3
	cycle straight down . Canute <u>Road</u>	and straight off the <u>prom</u>	into the <u>sea</u>		4
	– because we um	. we d make sure the tide was <u>sort</u> of in	. but you	5
	had to get rid of your <u>bike</u>	in mid <u>air</u>		6
C:	but didn t you do that dreadful <u>thing</u>	. to that <u>boy</u>		7
A:	o <u>yeah</u>		8
C:	where you were all kneeling <u>down</u>	as (xx)	9
A:	it s about an eight or ten foot <u>dive</u>	. <u>in</u>	and you can <u>dive</u>	at high <u>tide</u>		10
	. and Gus Hughes . came along one <u>day</u>	. and we were <u>al</u>ways taking	11
	the mickey out of him	. he s . you know	he s one of these . the lads	12
	that . <u>al</u>ways got taken	so we all . we all knelt <u>down</u>	– with the water up	13
	to about <u>there</u>	. he stood on the <u>top</u>	and said . is it o k to <u>dive</u>	we said	14
	<u>yes</u>	– but of course it was only about knee <u>deep</u>	– and he <u>dived</u>	. and	15
	he <u>stuck</u>	– he just went <u>crunch</u>		16

Directives

Communicative functions that involve influencing someone's action are sometimes called 'directives' or instances of 'suasion'. If the speaker feels that they have authority to get another person to do something, like parent with child, boss with employee, policeman in a crowd, or a professor with a flower girl, etc. – i.e. feel *dominance* – they use a fall. If the speaker does not feel they have authority but leaves the other person to decide, they use a rise – in *deference*. In this way, for instance, a **command** carries a falling tone, but a **request** a rise; for a request to be truly regarded as a request, the speaker has to allow the other person to decide to act or not. Compare these commands and requests:

10.46 i   I want you back at \underline{nine} (a command)

ii can you be back at /\underline{nine} (a request)

and

10.47 i   be back at \nine (a command)
       ii be back at /nine (a request)

Also compare these other contrasts in dominance (\) and deference (/):

10.48 i   don't argue with your \mother (a prohibition)
       ii don't argue with your /mother (a plea)

also

10.49 i   come \on (a demand)
       ii come /on (coaxing)

and

10.50 i   check your \watch (advice)
       ii check your /watch (suggestion)

and

10.51 i   you should check your \watch (advice)
       ii you could check your /watch (suggestion)

and

10.52 i   you could go with your \sister (recommendation)
       ii would you like to go with your /sister (invitation)

and

10.53 i   I'll be back at \nine (a promise)
       ii I could be back before /then (an offer)

also

10.54 i   don't you \dare be late (a threat)
       ii you shouldn't talk like /that (an appeal)

and finally

10.55 i   \watch it (a threat)
       ii /watch it (a warning)

Notice that, like requests, pleas, coaxing, suggestions, invitations, offers, appeals and warnings – if they are to be genuine – allow the addressee to decide; they could refuse a request, but not a command; they could go along with a plea, but they would have no choice with a prohibition; they could resist any coaxing, but not a demand; advice, recommendations and threats come with authority, but suggestions, invitations, appeals and warnings allow the addressee to make the final decision to act or not. Promises come with moral commitment; offers give the addressee options. Authority, or dominance, is signalled with the fall; deference to the addressee's right to decide is signalled with a rise.

However, if a more formal lexicalized expression of the communicative function is used, a fall is used.

10.56   I m putting in a request for a day \off |
I plead with you for \help |
I suggest ten \pounds |
we would like to invite you for a \meal |
our offer is on the \table |
we ap\peal to you |
I m \warning you |

Social interaction

Communicative functions for social interaction also differentiate between dominance and deference. Dominance in social interaction is the expression of the speaker's own feelings and is signalled by a fall; deference is a consideration of the addressee's feelings and is signalled by a rise. Consider the difference in **greetings**:

10.57   i   good \morning (formal, i.e. speaker's feelings dominate)
ii   good /morning (friendly, i.e. speaker considers the addressee's feelings)

and also

10.58   nice to /see you (friendly, thinking of the addressee)

Farewells:

10.59   i   good \bye (firm, command-like)
ii   good /bye (friendly, thinking of the addressee)

and

10.60   i   good \night (firm, command-like)
ii   good /night (friendly, thinking of the addressee)

also

10.61   good \riddance (firm, command-like; it does not seem possible with the more friendly rise!)

and

10.62   cheeri/o (friendly, thinking of the addressee)

see you /soon (friendly, thinking of the addressee)

Thanks:

10.63   i   many \thanks | \thank you (formal)
ii   many /thanks | /thank you (friendly, thinking of the addressee)

Congratulations and wishes:

10.64 i   well \done | congratu\lations (formal)
ii   well /done | congratu/lations (friendly, thinking of the addressee)

also

10.65 to the bride and \groom (formal)

and

10.66 i   happy \birthday (formal)
ii   happy /birthday (friendly, a genuinely good wish)

and

10.67 all the /best | have a nice /time (good wishes)

Praise:

10.68 \excellent | it's \brilliant

10.69 you shouldn't have \gone to so much trouble

Apologies, sympathy, regret:

10.70 /sorry | I beg your /pardon
I do a/pologize
sorry about /that | awfully /sorry
\sorry

Responses:

The following responses express the speaker's feelings with falls:

10.71 o \k
al\right
right you \are
I sup\pose so
if you in\sist

They can be contrasted with expressions of **concession, acquiescence** and **reassurance**, which take rises to signal the speaker's considerations of the addressee's feelings:

10.72 o /k
al/right
right you /are
I sup/pose so
if you in/sist

and

you'll be all /right

172

Calls with a fall *require* attention:

10.73 \Paul ('you must listen to me!')
Melissa \Jones
\hey | \you
ex\cuse me
\waiter

with a rise, they *seek contact*:

10.74 /John ('Are you there?')
Me/lissa
/waiter

with a fall-rise they *seek attention*:

10.75 vJohn ('I need you!')
Mevlissa
exvcuse me
vnurse

Back channel

falls indicate the back chaneller's positive engagement with the main speaker;
rises indicate their willingness for the main speaker to continue; mid level
indicates nothing more than that the back chaneller is there:

10.76 \yeah | \no | \oh | \m
/yeah | /no | /oh | /m
-yeah | -no | -oh | -m

Now see if you can add the most appropriate tones to the ***Pygmalion*** passage.
Your tonality and tonicity analysis may be somewhat different to the following
because of differences in interpretation; and now your tone choices might be
different too. But you are the director!

HIGGINS	<u>Why</u> | this is the girl I jotted down last <u>night</u> | <u>She's</u> no use | Ive got <u>all</u>	1
	the records I want | of the Lisson Grove <u>lingo</u> | and I'm not going to waste	2
	another <u>cy</u>linder on it | [*To the girl*] Be <u>off</u> with you | I don't <u>want</u> you |	3
THE FLOWER GIRL	Don't you be so <u>saucy</u> | You aint heard what I <u>come</u> for yet |	4
	[*To Mrs Pearce, who is waiting at the door for further instructions*] Did	5
	you tell him I come in a <u>taxi</u> |	6
MRS PEARCE	<u>Non</u>sense girl | What do you think a gentleman like Mr Higgins	7
	<u>cares</u> | what you <u>came</u> in?	8
THE FLOWER GIRL	Oh, we <u>are</u> proud | He aint above giving <u>lessons</u> | not <u>him</u> | I heard	9
	him <u>say</u> so| <u>Well</u> | I aint come here to ask for any <u>compliment</u> | and if my	10
	money's not <u>good</u> enough | I can go else<u>where</u> |	11
HIGGINS	Good enough for <u>what</u> |	12

THE FLOWER GIRL	Good enough for <u>yə-oo</u> | Now you <u>know</u> | <u>dont</u> you | I'm coming	13
	to have <u>lessons</u> | <u>I</u> am |And to <u>pay</u> for em | <u>tə-oo</u> | make no mis<u>take</u> |	14
HIGGINS *(stupent)*	<u>Well</u> | [*Recovering his breath with a gasp*] What do you	15
	expect me to <u>say</u> to you |	16
THE FLOWER GIRL	<u>Well</u> | if you was a <u>gentle</u>man | you might ask me to sit <u>down</u>	17
	I think | Dont I tell you I'm bringing you <u>business</u> |	18
HIGGINS	<u>Pickering</u> | shall we ask this baggage to sit <u>down</u> | or shall we throw	19
	her out of the <u>win</u>dow |	20
THE FLOWER GIRL	[*running away in terror to the piano, where she turns at bay*]	
	<u>Ah-ah-oh-ow-ow-ow-oo</u> | [*Wounded and whimpering*] I wont be called a	21
	<u>bag</u>gage | when Ive offered to <u>pay</u> |like a <u>lady</u> |	22

*

Here is a new piece of spoken discourse. A group of people are trying to co-operate in assembling a cot for a baby. Generally speaking the the tonality and tonicity will not be too difficult for you to transcribe, but try the tones too.

10.77 *Doing a job*

A:	it should fit there cos it s not that big . I don t think	1
	(pause)	
B:	it s warm in here shall I turn that down	2
A:	we ve got the instructions . anyway	3
	(pause)	
C:	just put it by the window or something	4
	(pause)	
D:	d you want me to take that	5
	(pause)	
B:	ooh – then there s bedding for about ten people here	6
	(pause)	
D:	ah	7
A:	um I say . um . we ve got some more instructions	8
	(pause)	
A:	that bit there s the bottom	9
B:	d you know you went up to um Nottingham yesterday .	10
	and you still didn t take Rogers duvet	11
D:	well – I wouldn t have had time to take it in any case . haven t seen him	12
B:	does he know we ve got it	13
D:	no – ah look at that	14
B:	(*unclear*)	
C:	it s not as difficult as it . appears	15
A:	she says you ve got to twist these round . and it makes them solid or	16
	something	17

C:	and all this just for you	18
	(*sigh, chuckling*; pause)	
A:	there that s solid now	19
B:	I think I ve made it unsolid . sorry .	20
	I ve done it the wrong way round . have I	21

*

Further exercises on tone can be found in Baker (1981, 1982), Bradford (1988), O'Connor & Fletcher (1989), Bowen & Marks (1992), Taylor (1992), Gilbert (1993), Hewings (1993, 2004), Brazil (1994), Kelly (2000), Hancock (2003) and Cauldwell (2003).

11 Intonation: secondary tone

Secondary tones

Secondary tone refers to variations to the basic primary system of \, / and v, and also to levels and movements in the pretonic segment (i.e. pre-head and head). Variations to the primary system involve *degrees* of fall, rise and fall-rise and these variations indicate something of the speaker's *attitude* or *strength of feeling* in expressing their message. Such variations can easily be demonstrated by listening to three variations of the following statement:

11.1 i   they re coming on \Monday |
ii   they re coming on \Monday |
iii they re coming on ˌMonday |

The first is a plain statement; the second is that very same statement but expressed more strongly as if to correct the addressee's expectation; and the third is expressed more mildly as if to confirm the addressee's expectation.

The fall in ii above starts from a higher pitch, higher than the automatic adjustment explained on p. 160; in other words, the speaker has chosen to manipulate the adjustment to express *strength* of feeling. In iii above, the speaker manipulates the adjustment to a lower starting point for the fall to express *mildness*.

Listen yet again to the narratives that we have been examining, but this time listen for falls that are higher or lower than normal. Overwrite any fall with a higher starting point with / and any fall with a lower than normal starting point with ˌ.

8.7 *Dangerous childhood pranks 1*

A: |my cousin \Mervin | . that was in the \REME | . uh . got me a thirty \eight   1
B: | \gun | 2
A: \Wesson | . Smith and \Wesson | . \special | . and \Benny's | . no it \wasn t | 3
it was Rick \Holmans's shed | . and \Benny | . Brian \Beddingfields | .   4
knew his dad had some . ammuˌnition | . from the \war | . and he \found   5
it | and they were thirty \eight | . so we um . took them over the   6
\marshes | and shot a couple of \rounds off | and that was \great | and   7
then one . | one day we were in up Prospect \Road | . near the \scout   8
hut | . in a \shed | . in a . um Rick \Holmans's shed | . so there was \four   9
of us | in this . sort of eight by s . six \shed | – - and we were   10

176

playing about with the \thing | . and we messed a\/bout with it | and did   11
the \usu you know | and and sort of said oh we ll put a \cross in it | 12
and make a \dum-dum of it | . and \fired it | . in the \shed | . at . at at the   13
bit of \wood | (*laughter*) . and this bullet went round the \shed | about   14
three \times | . and we all just \froze | . (*laughter*) and this bullet went   15
\round | and \round | and \round | (*laughter*) was absolutely out\rageous | 16
.and we had no \concept | of what we what could have \happened | 17

You might possibly have heard *gun* with a high fall, as speaker B tries to help speaker A out and does so with a touch of surprise. Line 6 *eight* seems higher than normal and sounds as if it conveys the speaker's surprise that the ammunition fitted the gun, perhaps unexpectedly. Line 9 *Holmans's* sounds low as if the name was well known to his addressees. Line 13 has *fired* high as if to express the speaker's feeling that this action would be opposite to the addressees' expectations, and *shed* likewise. Line 15 has *froze* high as the speaker emphasizes the participants' shock at what happened. *Outrageous* (line 16) is typical of those words with a powerful meaning and will often take a high tone. The high tone on *concept* (line 17) expresses the speaker's sense of incredulity.

The 'meaning' of the high fall has been glossed by other authors variously as 'intense', 'personal concern', 'involvement', 'liveliness', 'more emotional', 'surprise', 'strong surprise', 'vigorous agreement or contradiction'. This kind of variety of 'meanings' depends very much on other contributory factors like the speaker's choice of lexis, their gestures and situational factors. For instance, this statement

11.2   it s the po\lice

might express 'surprise', or in another situation 'great relief', or in yet another 'shock'! Facial gestures like wide opened eyes, eyes closed, frowns, smiles, pouts and a wrinkled up nose, and vocal gestures like loudness, whisper, speed, breathy or creaky voice all contribute also to 'meaning'. However, the contribution of the high fall is simply *strength of feeling*.

Similarly, the low fall has been glossed as 'cool', 'calm', 'phlegmatic', 'detached', 'reserved', 'dispassionate', 'dull', 'possibly grim', 'surly', 'unexcited', but once again, the exact description would depend on the accompanying lexis, gestures and situational factors. In general terms, the contribution of the low fall simply indicates *mildness of feeling*. Thus there is a threefold system of attitudinal expression:

\so   strong
\so   neutral
\so   mild

A further addition to this system is the rise-fall. The rise-fall consists of both a rise and then a fall on the tonic syllable. Remember that with an ordinary fall, there is usually a 'jump up' from the pitch of the end of the pretonic to a higher starting pitch of the fall; see p. 160. In the case of the rise-fall, the speaker manipulates this 'jump up' by 'vocalizing' it as a rise. Thus

11.3   i   it s the po^lice

expresses a greater level of surprise, etc. If the rise-fall is pitched low, this intense expression is increased with a greater sense of awe or shock. It is usually accompanied by breathy voice quality:

ii it s the po_^lice

Thus the whole system with falls is:

_^so	intense, with emotion
^so	intense
\so	strong
\so	neutral
_\so	mild

The attitudinal system with rises is simpler. What is most noticeable is the extent of the rise, either to a higher pitch than normal, or to a lower pitch:

11.4   i   they re coming on /Monday | . . .
        ii   they re coming on /Monday |
        iii they re coming on _/Monday |

The first rendering, i above, is a plain statement with incomplete information. The second, ii, is a challenge (look back at p. 167), with the purpose of seeking confirmation of what the addressee has just said. The third, iii, with a low rise, sounds either non-committal or even grudging, with quite a negative 'ring' to it. These three renderings can be matched with *yes/no* questions:

11.5   i   are they coming on /Monday |
        ii   are they coming on /Monday |
        iii are they coming on _/Monday |

The first rendering, i, is a plain *yes/no* question. The second, ii, is the very same question with strong feeling, e.g. surprise ('I didn't know that'). The third, iii, has the same negative 'ring' as 11.4iii. So the system so far can be set out as follows:

/so	strong
/so	neutral
_/so	non-committal

The categories are similar but with the reverse direction of the pitch movement, and so it might be tempting to extend the system to include the reverse of the rise-fall with questions, i.e. the fall-rise. But the fall-rise with *yes/no* questions has already briefly been mentioned (pp. 163–4) as indicating a focus of information, rather than the expression of an attitude. But there *is* an extension to the above system, with the inclusion of a mid level tone.

Mid level tones are usually non-final, and so fit neatly alongside the rise for incomplete information. The 'meaning' of the mid level tone has been glossed as 'marking non-finality without conveying any expression of expectancy', 'routine', 'bored', 'pre-coded', 'oblique'. It occurs in inventories and routine announcements; it often accompanies marked theme without attempting to make it prominent, simply 'syntactic dependence'. Here are some examples:

11.6   –Monday | –Tuesday | –Wednesday | –Thursday | \Friday
–Newport | Bristol –Parkway | –Swindon | –Reading | and London \Paddington
on –Monday | she goes to \Bristol | on –Tuesday | she goes to \Swansea | . . .

When preceded by a low head/pretonic, the mid level tone gives the impression of a kind of routine listing. Compare these two renderings of a list:

11.7   i   they re coming on /Monday | staying on /Tuesday | and /Wednesday | and
\Thursday |
ii   they re coming on –Monday | staying on –Tuesday | and –Wednesday |
and –Thursday | as they ˌalways do |

Thus the mid level tone 'means' something like 'as is well known', hence the glosses 'pre-coded' and 'routine'. The system then is:

/so   strong
/so   neutral
–so   routine
ˌso   non-committal

The fall-rise has a low variety, matching the low rise-fall described above, with a matching effect: implied information with strong emotion. Like the low rise-fall, it is often accompanied by breathy voice. Compare:

11.8   i   they re coming on vMonday |
ii   they re coming on ˌMonday |

also

I suppose we ll have to call the poˌlice |

There is just a two item system:

vso   neutral
ˌso   intense, with emotion

These are all the variations to the basic, primary, tones – the secondary tones in the tonic segment.

Heads and pre-heads

We now turn to the variations in the head and pre-head – the secondary tones in the pretonic segment. The simplest kind of variation is to change the general pitch level of the head to either higher than normal, or to lower:

11.9 i   they re coming on \Mon̲day |
     ii   ⁻they re coming on \Mon̲day |
     iii   _they re coming on \Mon̲day |

The second rendering, ii above, has a high level head and sounds more 'insist-ent'. The third, iii, with a low level head, means given information, i.e. infor-mation treated as already known by the addressee, before a narrow focus (see p. 152). The system is then:

unmarked   neutral
     ⁻so . . .   intense
     _so . . .   given

Instead of remaining level, the pitch may descend gradually through the head, a so-called 'falling head', or it may ascend, a 'rising head'. Such a movement adds an element of 'warmth'; that 'warmth' is combined with a sense of author-ity if the movement is downwards, and with a sense of appeal if it is upwards. Compare:

11.10 i   they ll ↓ all be coming on \Mon̲day | (i.e. 'I can assure you')
     ii   they ll ↗ all be coming on \Mon̲day | (i.e. 'I appeal to you; believe me')
(Note that the arrow accents appear in the head; they do **not** accompany the tonic.)

Instead of a relatively smooth descent or ascent, the movement can 'step' grad-ually downwards or upwards; this so-called 'stepping head' adds a sense of emphasis combined with either authority or appeal:

iii they ll ↓ all be ↓coming on \Mon̲day | (i.e. 'I emphatically assure you')
iv   they ll ↗ all be ↑coming on \Mon̲day | (i.e. 'I strongly appeal to you; believe me')

Instead of a general movement downwards or upwards in the head, there may be a series of movements; this so-called 'glissando head' adds forcefulness:

v   they ll ↓ all be ↓ coming on \Mon̲day | (i.e. 'I have told you many times')
vi they ll ↗ all be ↗ coming on \Mon̲day | (i.e. 'I have told you many times; I beg you to believe me')

If there is no head, but just a pre-head, a limited system can operate:

11.11 i   the po\li̲ce | (neutral, as if announcing a heading or sub-heading in a talk)
     ii   ⁻the po\li̲ce | (intense)

The full secondary tone system for the pretonic segment is as follows:

so	neutral	(unmarked)
⁻so . . .	high level	'intense'
_so . . .	low level	given
↓so . . .	falling	warm, with authority
↗so . . .	rising	warm, with appeal

180

↓so ↓so . . .	stepping down	emphatic, with authority
↗so ↑so . . .	stepping up	emphatic, with appeal
↓so↓so . . .	glissando down	forceful, with authority
↗so↗so . . .	glissando up	forceful, with appeal

It must, of course, be understood that there may be more than two stressed syllables in the head, thus, for instance: ↓↓↓, or ↗↗↗, etc.

It must also be understood that neutral and secondary pretonics can combine with any primary or secondary tones in the tonic segment, allowing, theoretically, for a vast number of combinations; but there are certain combinations that are more frequent than others. Listen to these:

11.12   if they re↓all going to come on /<u>Mon</u>day   (warm, incomplete)

↗how are we going to \<u>sleep</u> them   (warm, with appeal)

they ll↓have to ↓bring at ↓least a v<u>camp</u>ing bed (emphatic, with implication)

I just ↗hope they ve ↑still \<u>got</u> it   (emphatic, with appeal, i.e. need to find out)

well I↓hope they↓have nt got v<u>rid</u> of it   (forceful, with implication)

do you ↗think we can ↗ask them to /<u>bring</u> it   (forceful, with appeal, i.e. to agree to the question)

Now try your directing expertise on the **Pygmalion** passage, and edit the transcription you did on pp. 173–4.

*

Very little practice material seems to exist for secondary tones, apart from Brazil (1994) and Cauldwell (2003) on the mid level tone.

12 Intonation: paratones

Paratones

Spoken discourse exhibits the kinds of structure that written discourse is seen to have: sentences, paragraphs, sections and sub-sections, chapters and the sense of a whole 'document' or book. A para*graph* is something *written*; the equivalent in speech has been termed a 'para*tone*' – a phonological paragraph. Paratones tend to be shorter than paragraphs and may often be more equivalent to extended sentences. Paratones also extend over sequences of speaker turns in conversations.

Just as paragraphs are used for new topics, shifts in temporal sequence or episodic events, we use paratones for similar purposes. A very clear example is the reading of the news: each new topic is distinguished from a previous one by intonation – the newsreader normally indicates that they are introducing a new news item simply by a change in intonation. Narratives, whether scripted or spontaneous, are structured intonationally in similar ways. It may be rather more difficult to perceive such structure in casual, informal conversation because of the way it is composed, but structures are there nevertheless. The key to these phonological paragraphs – paratones – have been listed as follows:

1. a high pitch on the onset syllable of the initial intonation unit in the paratone;
2. a relatively high 'baseline' for that initial unit; this means that the low pitches are relatively high, compared to the low pitches in the final unit of the paratone;
3. there is a gradual lowering – or 'declination' – of the baseline as the paratone progresses until the final unit is reached;
4. the depth of the fall in the final unit is the lowest in the whole paratone;
5. there is usually a slowing down process in the final unit, so-called 'pre-boundary lengthening'; and
6. there is usually a longer pause than is normally allowed between intonation units within a paratone.

Listen now again to **Dangerous childhood pranks** 1 and see if you can hear paratone boundaries; mark them with a double upright: ||. As we have noted before, not all features need to be present for signalling an item in intonation, but listen especially for a low 'baseline' pitch, a pause and a relatively high pitch in the following unit in lines 3, 5, 6, 7, 9, 10, 15, 16 and 17.

8.7 *Dangerous childhood pranks* 1

A: |my cousin \Mervin | . that was in the \REME | . uh . got me a thirty \eight   1
B: | \gun | 2
A: \Wesson | . Smith and \Wesson | . \special || . and \Benny's | . no it \wasn t | 3
it was Rick \Holmans's shed | . and \Benny | . Brian \Beddingfields | .   4
knew his dad had some . ammu\nition | . from the \war ||. and he \found   5
it | and they were thirty \eight || . so we um . took them over the   6
\marshes | and shot a couple of \rounds off | and that was \great || and   7
then one . | one day we were in up Prospect \Road | . near the \scout   8
hut | . in a \shed | . in a . um Rick \Holmans's shed || . so there was \four   9
of us | in this . sort of eight by s . six \shed || – and we were   10
playing about with the /thing | . and we messed a\/bout with it | and did   11
the \usu you know | and and sort of said oh we ll put a \cross in it | 12
and make a \/dum-dum of it | . and \fired it | . in the \shed | . at . at at the   13
bit of \wood | (*laughter*) . and this bullet went round the \shed | about   14
three \times || . and we all just \froze | . (*laughter*) and this bullet went   15
\round | and \round | and \round | (*laughter*) was absolutely out\rageous || 16
.and we had no \concept | of what we what could have \happened || 17

See if you can find the paratone boundaries in ***Dangerous childhood pranks* 2**.

⋆

Declination, the gradual descent of the baseline from the initial intonation unit in a paratone to the final unit, is an effective way of indicating that the units do in fact belong to each other, and could be regarded as the neutral form. But the declination could be interrupted; and this is a decision by the speaker. The speaker might decide to halt the declination by raising the pitch of the onset of the following unit, or by dropping it to a lower than expected level.

If the speaker raises the baseline in the course of a paratone, instead of allowing it to descend gradually, it usually means that they are introducing a piece of information that is contrary to what might have been otherwise expected; in some way, the information is deemed to be contrastive. Examples occur in ***Dangerous childhood pranks* 1** line 13. The speaker initiates a paratone at line 10 and does not seem to finish it until line 15 with a 'deep' fall on *times*. But in the course of this paratone, he raises the baseline twice, on . *and fired it* and . *in the shed*. He realizes that people would not expect them to fire the gun, and especially not in such a small shed; hence the 'contrastive' nature of the information. We could transcribe this raising of the baseline as follows: ⌉

- ⌉ . and \`fired ⌉ . in the \`shed |

If the speaker maintains the pitch level of the baseline, instead of allowing it to descend gradually, it usually means that they are introducing a piece of information that is equivalent to the information that they have just supplied.

Listen, for example, to lines 5 and 6; the baseline of *and he found it* is maintained in *and they were thirty eight*, indicating that the speaker regards the second piece of information as equivalent to the previous piece. We could transcribe this maintaining of the baseline as ꟷ:

- | . and he found it ꟷ and they were thirty \eight ||

Finally, if the speaker dropped the pitch level of the onset syllable and the baseline to a lower level than expected, it usually means that the speaker either wishes to indicate that the next piece of information is fully expected, or that the next piece of information should be regarded as a parenthesis. Listen, for example, firstly to line 3, where the speaker corrects himself with *no it wasn't*, as a parenthesis, on a lower than otherwise expected pitch level and then provides the corrected information about *Rick Holmans's shed*; and then listen, secondly, to line 9 where mention is made again of *Rick Holmans's shed*, and because that information is fully known, it is pitched on a lower than expected level. We can transcribe this dropping of the baseline as ⌐:

- || . \Benny's ⌐ no it \wasn t |
- | . in a \shed ⌐ in a . um Rick \Holmans's shed ||

You will be able to find similar examples in **Dangerous childhood pranks** 2, but there are two particularly interesting examples in lines 14 and 15. There the speaker reports direct speech, and does so with a raised baseline. His words *and said* and *we said* are pitched low as pre-heads – although *said* is a lexical item, it is certainly not stressed – and then the direct speech is pitched on a higher than expected baseline *within* the intonation unit. One possible way of transcribing this is to enclose the 'raised baseline' symbol within brackets, (⌐):

- | and said . (⌐) is it o k to /dive | we said (⌐) \yes ||

That leads to a consideration of another change in intonation patterns taking place in UK at present (one change was mentioned on p. 164). There is a relatively new pattern that has been often referred to as the 'high rising terminal' ('HRT'); a better term is a 'raised rise'. A person can be telling a story, a joke or some kind of narrative, and check whether the addressee has understood the significance of a particular piece of information. They provide the addressee with new information, in a declarative clause, but at the same time, ask whether they realize the significance of it; in other words, they are, at that moment, doing two things at the same: telling and asking. This is accomplished by retaining the declarative mood, choosing a rising tone, but choosing also a higher baseline – as in the above case of introducing direct speech. Listen to this description of a speaker's visit to a craft fair in Cambridge, especially for the instance of a raised rise where the speaker seems to be telling her addresses something new, but checking at the same time if they know what she means:

12.1   *Cambridge craft fair*

oh what did I see what did I see . stained glass – there was I went	1
to a craft fair – – um in Cambridge . and um . I know – I went	2
to a craft fair in Cambridge and they had . um this stained glass stall	3
. and it was all mobiles . made out of stained glass – and they were	4
superb they were . and mirrors . with all different colours . like going	5
round in . the colour . colour wheel – but all different sized bits of	6
coloured glass on it	7

In lines 5 and 6, she talks about coloured mirrors that go round in a colour wheel; *going round in the colour wheel* is new information, but she seems to want to check with her addressees at the same time that they know what a *colour wheel* is. (A *colour wheel*, apparently, is a circular chart used by artists, which shows the relationship between the different colours in the spectrum; it is a compound noun.)

This is a very clever innovation. It provides new information in a declarative clause; it asks a question with a rising tone; it interrupts the course of the pitch movement in the intonation unit by introducing a raised baseline, like the direct speech above. It is different from the declarative with a rising tone described on p. 167 as a challenge. Challenges refer back immediately as a response to what has just been said; and there is no raising of the baseline. But statement-verifications of this kind do not refer back to previous information; they contribute new information in the development of the discourse. We can transcribe lines 5 and 6 as follows:

- \mirrors | . with all different \colours | . like going round in . the colour . (↑)/colour wheel |

You can attempt the transcription of the tonality, tonicity and tone of the rest of this little monologue.

Calling

There is just one other pattern of intonation that needs to be mentioned. Sometimes we need to call out a short message over a distance, like *Dinner's ready!* There is a special kind of pattern for this kind of *calling*. They are very short paratones, consisting of a single intonation unit with a two-level tone: high level and then mid level, which is maintained through the tail. If there is no tail, the two-level tone may even distort the tonic syllable by prolonging it, to make time for the change in pitch. Listen to these callings:

12.2   ‾dinner s –ready || come and ‾get –it || it s on the ‾tab–le || come ‾o–on ||

The usual features of paratone boundaries do not seem to apply in the case of *calling*. Callings do, of course, come singly as well as in sequences as above! Listen to this one!

12.3   we v ‾fin–ished ||

*

For a little more practice material, see Bradford (1988), Brazil (1994), Hancock (2003) and Cauldwell (2003).

*

12.4   /<u>now</u> | we \<u>have</u> finished |

This concludes one of the most comprehensive guides to intonation transcription currently in print!

And that means that there are now no words or pieces of discourse that you cannot transcribe!

BIBLIOGRAPHY

Part I Words . . .

Ashby, P. (2005) *Speech Sounds.* 2nd edn. London: Routledge.

Collins, B. & Mees, I. M. (2003) *Practical Phonetics and Phonology.* London: Routledge.

Fletcher, C. (1990) *Longman Pronunciation Dictionary Study Guide.* London: Longman.

Garcia Lecumberri, M. L. & Maidment, J. A. (2000) *English Transcription Course.* London: Arnold.

Gimson, A. C. (2008) *Gimson's Pronunciation of English.* 7th edn. Rev. by Cruttenden, A. London: Hodder.

International Phonetic Association (1999) *Handbook of the International Phonetic Association.* Cambridge University Press.

Kenworthy, J. (2000) *The Pronunciation of English: A Workbook.* London: Arnold.

Kreidler, C. W. (1997) *Describing Spoken English.* London: Routledge.

  (2004) *The Pronunciation of English: A Coursebook.* Malden MA: Blackwell.

Ladegoged, P. (2001) *A Course in Phonetics.* 4th edn. Boston: Heinle & Heinle.

Roach, P. (2009) *English Phonetics and Phonology.* 4th edn. Cambridge University Press.

Shockey, L. (2003) *Sound Patterns of Spoken English* Oxford: Blackwell.

Wells, J. C. (1982) *Accents of English.* 3 volumes. Cambridge University Press.

Wells, J. C. & Colson, G. (1971) *Practical Phonetics.* London: Pitman.

And these three dictionaries:

Jones, D. (2006) *English Pronouncing Dictionary.* 17th edn. Edited by Roach, P., Hartman, J. & Setter, J. Cambridge University Press.

Upton, C., Kretzschmar, W. A. & Konopka, R. (2001) *The Oxford Dictionary of Pronunciation for Current English.* Oxford University Press.

Wells, J. C. (2008) *Longman Pronunciation Dictionary.* 3rd edn. London: Longman.

Part II . . . and Discourse

Much of the literature on rhythm will be found in the works listed above in Part I. This list relates to intonation.

Intonation description

Beckman, M. E. & Elam, G. A. (1997) *Guidelines for ToBI Labeling.* Version 3. Ohio State University.

Brazil, D. (1975) *Discourse Intonation.* English Language Research, University of Birmingham.

 (1997) *The Communicative Value of Intonation in English.* Cambridge University Press.

Cruttenden, A. (1997) *Intonation.* 2nd edn. Cambridge University Press.

Crystal, D. (1969) *Prosodic Systems and Intonation in English.* Cambridge University Press.

 (1975) *The English Tone of Voice.* London: Arnold.

Gussenhoven, C. (2004) *The Phonology of Tone and Intonation.* Cambridge University Press.

Halliday, M. A. K. (1967) *Intonation and Grammar in British English.* The Hague: Mouton.

 (1970) *A Course in Spoken English: Intonation.* Oxford University Press.

Halliday, M. A. K. & Greaves, W. S. (2008) *Intonation in the Grammar of English.* London: Equinox.

Ladd, D. R. (1996) *Intonational Phonology.* Cambridge University Press.

Pierrehumbert, J. B. (1987) *The Phonology and Phonetics of English Intonation.* Indiana University.

Pike, K. L. (1945) *The Intonation of American English.* Ann Arbor: University of Michigan Press.

Tench, P. (1996a) *The Intonation Systems of English.* London: Cassell.

 (1996b) 'Intonation and the differentiation of syntactic patterns in English and German'. *International Journal of Applied Linguistics* 6:2.

 (2003) 'Processes of semogenesis in English intonation'. *Functions of Language* 10:2.

 (ed.) (2005) Intonation: Ways and Meanings (with cd). *Speak Out! 34.*

Wells, J. C. (2006) *English Intonation: An Introduction.* Cambridge University Press.

Intonation practice

Beer, H. (2005) Overcoming Ambiguities in Spoken English. *Speak Out! 34.*

Baker, A. (1981) *Ship or Sheep?* 2nd edn. Cambridge University Press.

 (1982) *Tree or Three?* Cambridge University Press.

Bowen, T. & Marks, J. (1992) *The Pronunciation Book*. Harlow: Longman.

Bradford, B. (1988) *Intonation in Context*. Cambridge University Press.

Brazil, D. (1994) *Pronunciation for Advanced Learners of English*. Cambridge University Press.

Cauldwell, R. (2003) *Streaming Speech*. Birmingham: Speechinaction.

Gilbert, J. B. (1993) *Clear Speech*. 2nd edn. New York: Cambridge University Press.

Hancock, M. (2003) *English Pronunciation in Use*. Cambridge University Press.

Hewings, M. (1993) *Pronunciation Tasks*. Cambridge University Press.

(2004) *Pronunciation Practice Activities*. Cambridge University Press.

Kelly, G. (2000) *How to Teach Pronunciation*. Harlow: Longman.

O'Connor, J. D. & Fletcher, C. (1989) *Sounds English*. Harlow: Longman.

Taylor, L. (1992) *Pronunciation in Action*. Hemel Hempstead: Prentice Hall.

INDEX

(Please note that f stands for the discussion that follows, whereas hyphenated numbers stand for single references.)